FATHER FORGIVE THEM

THE RACHEL PLUMMER STORY

Garlyn Webb Wilburn

[signature: Garlyn Wilburn]

Black Rose Writing

www.blackrosewriting.com

The final approval for this literary material is granted by the author.

First printing

The story of Rachel Parker Plummer is true and actual, but recounted in fictional form. Its' historical facts have been researched and well documented. With some exceptions, conversation is fiction (for only a few are recorded in the narratives of Rachel and her father) but is relative in keeping with attitudes and character as the author could gain through plausible research.

ISBN: 978-1-61296-087-6

PUBLISHED BY BLACK ROSE WRITING

www.blackrosewriting.com

Printed in the United States of America

Father Forgive Them is printed in Times New Roman

Introduction

On Thursday, May 19, 1836, just twenty-eight days after Texas won her independence from Mexico, an Indian raiding party of around four hundred Comanche and Kiowa warriors, attacked a civilian fortress in central Texas called 'Fort Parker' (near the present town of Groesbeck, Texas). Five men were killed in the onslaught, five people taken captive, and the rest, some twenty-seven men, women and children, managed to flee to the Navasota River bottom and hide in briar-covered thickets.

After plundering and ransacking the fort the Indians placed their five prisoners, three children and two women, on horseback and sped away leaving behind a holocaust of devastation. Soon the warriors would divide the captives, then travel in different directions to confuse any pursuers.

In the early days of Texas colonization, scenes such as this were not uncommon. For two hundred years it had been the practice of the Comanche to raid Mexican villages taking women and children captives to become slaves. With the great increase of white American settlers pouring into the Mexican province of Texas during the early 1800's raiding Indian bands found an easy marked prey. In later years some captives would be ransomed and returned to their people, but a far greater number of unfortunate victims spent the remainder of their lives among the Indians.

Such could be the fate awaiting the five prisoners taken at Fort Parker, whose families chose to intrude far into the sparsely settled wilderness of Texas – Comanche territory.

Table of Contents

Father Forgive Them

The Rachel Plummer Story

Texas
Thursday, May 19, 1836

The morning fog had now lifted, giving way to a clear day. Fanned by a soft breeze wisps of smoke, rising from the sizzling fires beneath cast-iron tubs, drifted lazily across the compound and over the fort's twelve-foot high log walls to mingle with the gentle fragrances of flowering bluebonnets and dogwood blossoms.

Standing barefoot in the doorway of her cabin, seventeen-year-old Rachel Plummer dusted her flour covered hands on a frayed apron and watched her eighteen-month-old son, James Pratt, play happily in the sandy earth. Later she would pour the raw kneaded dough into cast-iron pans to be placed in smoldering embers left by earlier fires. Soon the flavorful aroma of freshly baked bread, for the noon meal, would fill the air.

Rachel, fair and youthful, with rosy cheeks, red hair and a sprinkling of freckles across her delicate nose, was a delightful young lady, but occasionally could be a little headstrong.

Brushing away strands of silky hair from her brow, she shaded her eyes against the glare of the mid-morning sun and watched her two aunts, Lucy Parker and Elizabeth Kellogg, as they labored over steaming tubs. Bending over the hot sudsy wash pots, they scrubbed dirt and grime from the well-worn clothing.

Earlier that morning Rachel had eased out of bed and in the pre-dawn light slipped out of her nightgown and into a faded flower-print dress. With eggs in one hand and skillet in the other she sleepily stumbled out of the cabin into the damp sultry air. Her mother, Patsey, and older sister, Sarah, were already up frying cornmeal bread for the men's breakfast, over orange glowing coals left by last night's campfire.

"Well! Have you told him yet?" her mother questioned, as Rachel approached the fire.

"Uh-huh."

"Well!"

"What are you talking about, Mama?" Sarah asked.

"Oh, Rachel is three months pregnant and hasn't told Luther yet." Luther was Rachel's husband.

"What did he say when you told him?" Sarah asked her younger sister. "Was he excited?"

"Umm, uh-huh. I guess so. He just smiled and said he had been wondering why Elder John was working on a baby cradle."

"He never seems to get too excited about anything," Sarah remarked.

Luther, a muscular, hardworking young man with square shoulders and large calloused hands had married Rachel when she was fifteen and he was twenty-four. He and Sarah's husband, Lorenzo, planned to leave for the cornfield by good daybreak. With the help of Rachel's father, James, and eight-year-old brother, James Wilson they reasoned that by leaving early and working hard, they could finish hoeing the field before dark.

Seventy-five-year-old Elder John Parker closed his bible and set it down beside him. He had been setting on a log in the middle of the fort compound since daylight reading scripture. In front of him set the unfinished crafting of a baby cradle made of willow limbs. Slowly John picked up a small limber branch and began to weave it into the cradle.

Elder John, a thickset man with silver hair and beard and a wrinkled, stern-looking face, was the patriarch of the Parker clan and Elder of their church. On Sundays, while his son, James, preached the morning service, he sat rigidly in front wearing a crisp white shirt and black coat, looking out over his congregation.

With a small child in-tow, Elder John's wife shuffled over to the log, removed her sunbonnet and plopped down beside him. Placing two-year-old Silas Jr. on her lap, Granny awkwardly thumbed open

2

her bible and began reading aloud.

The fort was a lively place this late spring morning. Men and women bustling around, hard at work. Samuel Frost and his son Robert were roofing a cabin with hand-hewn shingles. At the far end of the compound Silas Parker and his brother Benjamin were shoeing horses. Older children busied themselves feeding animals, gathering eggs, milking cows, and other chores.

This was Fort Parker, a sanctuary in the wild, sparsely-settled wilderness of central Texas – Indian country. Constructed in 1835 by the Parker extended family, which migrated from Illinois, it offered a protective cover as men and women went about their daily tasks and small children engaged in carefree play.

Twelve-foot high log walls enclosed the near two-acre compound with a lookout blockhouse erected at the northeast and southwest corners. Six small, one-room log cabins, with dirt floors and fireplaces were built against the inside walls. To the Parkers, the fortification seemed almost impregnable. A refuge of safety not only for its' thirty-four inhabitants but for the other families living nearby.

One month had passed since Texas won her independence from Mexico at the Battle of San Jacinto, freeing the people to establish a democratic government representing and protecting its' inhabitants. No longer threatened by an invasion from a relentless Mexican army, an atmosphere of serene peacefulness and security hung over the fort.

For a moment Rachel stood in the doorway listening as Granny struggled to read the biblical passages. With eyes growing dim with age she most likely recited more from memory than from reading the printed word.

Smiling within herself Rachel quickly checked her son then turned to go back inside. Hearing Granny's voice stop in mid scripture, she abruptly glanced back. Granny had set little Silas down and now stood transfixed, gazing over the west wall watching billows of dust floating high in the sky.

"Benjamin! Silas!" she shouted at her two sons. "You better get over here and see what's going on!"

The two men glanced up from their work and looked to the west where their mother was pointing. Seeing dust clouds drifting upward they threw down their tools and rushed toward the two large open gates.

By now everyone had stopped in what they were doing watching and wondering – even the children.

"What do you think it is?" Granny asked her husband anxiously.

"Hmm – could be a herd of buffalo but I don't hear – listen!"

The faint rhythmical drumming of many approaching horses could be heard.

"It's Indians!" Silas bellowed. "Hundreds of them! You women and children go hide in the woods! Sarah! Sarah Nixon! Go to the field and tell the men! Hurry!" His roaring voice rang over the compound sending people fleeing everywhere. All appeared to be in a state of confusion.

Not knowing where to go or what to do Rachel hesitated for a moment, watching mass bedlam unfold around her.

The large front gates stood wide open, swung back against the wall. Several men, who seemed spellbound, watched the approaching Indians gallop their mounts to within a hundred yards of the stockade and jerk them to an abrupt stop.

Driven by extreme fear, most women and children had scurried out the small back gate. Some scrambled to hide in the thick brush of the Navasota River bottom. Others raced for the cornfield to warn the men working there.

In a daze, Rachel grabbed up her son and fled toward the open gates in an attempt to escape. Upon reaching the opening she froze. Sitting some distance out, astride restless horses, were bare chested warriors too numerous to count. Terrified of being caught in her flight to the thick forest she stayed within the fort walls.

"What you reckon they want?" Silas said grimly.

"Those are Comanche and Kiowa, maybe four hundred or more. They're up to no good. You can count on that," Elder John replied.

"We'll know soon enough," Benjamin declared.

"Oh Dear God," Rachel murmured. "Lord please save us." She bent down on her knees peering at the scene outside through the small slit between the wall's upright logs. What she saw gripped her with fear and blood seemed to drain from her body.

4

Hundreds of paint-faced warriors on wiry mustangs watched while a lone rider approached the stockade. From his six-foot lance a white flag of truce fluttered in the morning breeze. All others sat motionless on their fidgety ponies while brightly colored feathers attached to shields and up-raised spears bobbed in the wind. Their thin hawk-faces were a mask of red paint slashed across cheeks and chins, with black rings around satanically peering eyes. A bow and quiver hung from bare chests.

Looking through the gap between the logs, Rachel watched as the Indian with the flag cantered his mount within twenty yards of the gates and yanked him to a stop.

"We come in peace!" the painted warrior announced loudly in broken English. "We wish to make a treaty with you!" All the time his blazing eyes scanned the inside of the fort.

"I'm going out to talk to them," Benjamin declared.

He was only gone for a few short minutes.

"I believe they intend to attack the fort," he told Silas and the other four men. "You best get ready. I'm going back to see if this fight can be avoided."

"Don't go! They'll kill you!" Silas warned. "Stay here and we'll defend the place as best we can."

"Wait Ben!" Samuel Frost urged. "Let's see what they're gon'na do. Dwight will be back in a moment." (G. E. Dwight had left with the women and children to hide them in the forest.) "I'm sure James and the other men working in the fields will be here shortly. Let's make a stand here."

Benjamin hesitated for a moment, then without a word, turned and trudged out toward the waiting multitude of intruders.

"They'll kill him for sure," Elder John muttered.

Rachel scooped up James Pratt in her arms and fled through the gate. Glancing back she let out a terror-stricken scream. The Indians had thrust their spears through Benjamin and were now shooting arrows into his body as he lay quivering on the ground.

"Run Rachel! Run! Get out of here!" her uncle Silas yelled.

Clutching James Pratt against her breast she took flight for the bottom land thicket only to be caught by two mounted shrieking savages and thrown to the ground, her baby snatched from her arms.

While trying desperately to retrieve her screaming son one of the paint-faced, sulky men picked up a hoe and clubbed her in the head, knocking her to the ground.

Horrifying howls and squalls pierced the morning air as hundreds of blood thirsty braves bolted their mounts and poured through the stockade's open gate, dealing out death to all within.

* * *

James Parker straightened up and leaned over on his hoe to rest. With a rag he mopped streams of sweat from his face and neck then glanced up at the glowing sun that had now inched high in the morning sky. He, his son and two men had been hoeing weeds and grass from their cornfield since early morning and were now only about a quarter of the way finished.

"Listen!" James shouted to the other men, holding up his hand. "There it is again!" a heart-stopping frantic cry rang out echoing through the woods.

"That's my wife Sarah!" Lorenzo Nixon yelled. "Something horrible must have happened! Let's go!"

Throwing down their hoes they raced toward the fort and the sound of Sarah's cry for help.

Staggering up to her husband Sarah fell to her knees, so out of breath and anxious she could scarcely utter a word. Choking back tears she managed to sputter "Indians! Indians at the fort!"

All started for the fort in hast but within a hundred yards they met up with James's terrified wife, Patsey, her two children and two grandchildren.

"Indians!" she gasped. "Hundreds of Indians! They have surrounded the fort."

"Luther! Hurry and alarm our neighbors!" James commanded desperately. "Lorenzo you head to the fort. I'm taking the women and children to the river bottom. I'll catch up with you."

* * *

When Rachel began to come out of a semi-conscious state she was seized by her long hair and dragged screaming back to the gate where Indian women, with clubs, were mutilating the lifeless bodies of Samuel Frost and his son Robert. Seeing Rachel they began pounding her with sticks, clubs and whips and continued thrashing her until she stopped screaming and lay motionless on the ground, bruised and bleeding.

While lying there on her stomach one of the filthy-smelling raiders tied her hands behind her back, then her feet.

Covered in dirt and drying streaks of blood Rachel struggled to a sitting position, and in a daze allowed her near swollen eyes to explore the horrid sight before her. Utter chaos now consumed the entire fort. Shrieks, whoops and piercing cries rang through the air as the invaders ran around like raging animals, plundering and ransacking the fort, tearing up everything in sight and throwing debris across the compound. Others plowed their wide-eyed ponies through the stock pens, scattering the frightened animals and chickens in all directions. Dust, along with feathers from ripped open mattresses, rose in billows from the ground. Not far from where Rachel was sitting lay the lifeless bodies of her uncle Silas and grandfather Elder John, both scalped and riddled with arrows. Nearby lay Granny Parker. She had been stabbed and stripped naked, but was not dead. Her pitiful moans were heart rending.

Fearful that he may have been killed, Rachel frantically searched the horrifying turmoil for her eighteen-month-old son. Seeing him held on a horse by his captor, wailing for his mother, she cried out, only to be whacked across the face with a whip.

* * *

Fleeing out the small back gate of the fort carrying two of her small children, Silas Parkers, wife, Lucy, struggled to herd the two older children swiftly along the path leading to the forest.

"Run Cynthia Ann! Take John's hand and run for the woods and hide!" she shouted anxiously. Close behind she could hear the pounding hoof beats of approaching horses, which quickly surrounded her and the children.

"Get away from us! Leave us alone!" Lucy screamed frantically while trying to hide her children with her long dress.

Four of the painted, warriors cantered their mounts within a few feet of the terrorized family and, with their threatening long lances pointed at Lucy, gesturing for her to hand over the children. With nine-year-old Cynthia Ann and five-year-old John clinging desperately to their mother, Lucy tried to back away, shaking her head in despair at the mask faced enemy.

Closing the circle around their prey, two warriors leaned from their ponies and snatched Cynthia and John up behind them. Whirling their mounts around, they dashed toward the fort with their captives screaming for their mother.

With sharp pointed lances prodding her, Lucy and her two babies were forced back toward the stockade.

Not far away unarmed Lorenzo Nixon, who had rushed from the field, arrived just in time to witness the horrifying scene. With his heart beating wildly he gave a bloodcurdling yell and charged the unsuspecting warriors who were trying to pry Lucy's babies from her grasp.

Just when the Indians were about to kill Lorenzo, David Faulkenberry, a close neighbor, appeared with his rifle, causing them to fall back.

Holding one child in her arm and leading the other Lucy scrambled toward David. While making their escape several mounted braves followed but retreated when they saw David's gun aimed at them.

Sobbing with grief for her captured children Lucy fled deeper and deeper into the heavy timber and safety.

* * *

Sometime before noon Elizabeth Kellogg was brought in. Bound by her hands, she was flung to the ground, beside Rachel, her feet were then tied and the Indian women commenced beating her with sticks.

"Don't cry out Elizabeth," Rachel said in a weak voice. "They'll only beat you more." Immediately she received lashings about the head.

The squaws continued to club Elizabeth until she was almost unconscious.

Hearing the whimpering and sobbing of children, Rachel looked up to see two mounted horses with Cynthia and John sitting in back of their painted captors.

Rachel tried to inch her way over near Elizabeth, who was now moaning, but received a blow, which knocked her back to the ground.

Not long afterwards the two women were jerked to their feet, their hands untied from behind and retied in front. After placing them on horses, squaws tied their feet together by a rope going under the horse's belly. It was in this position they rode from the fort, while shrieking Comanche warriors raced by on fiery mustangs displaying bloody scalps from their long upright lances.

As the large party of Indians and captives bound from the stockade, leaving behind a scene of holocaust devastation, Rachel glanced back at the place where just a few hours before she had been happy and free and now was being held in the clutches of merciless savages. It was at that moment she remembered again the dreadful stories told of women captives being tortured, gang raped and some even suffering a horrible slow death.

"Oh merciful Lord," Rachel prayed. "Deliver us from these hideous people. My Heavenly Father, why would you lead your faithful people to such a hostile wilderness?"

Memories of a peaceful, quiet, untroubled life, left behind in Illinois not many years past, flooded her mind. A place she yearned to return. A home she had not ever wanted to leave. A life she doubtfully would ever regain again.

Crawford County, Illinois
March 1833

"I'm not going to Texas," Rachel whispered to her sister, grimly. Sarah, who was two years older, tried to ignore her fourteen-year-old indignant sister.

They were standing at the back of the small overcrowded church listening to their uncle Daniel proclaim to the congregation the wonderful opportunities awaiting them in a place called 'Texas'. It was there that a family could homestead 4,600 acres in this vast, sparsely settled region.

Rachel's father, James Parker and her uncle Daniel had just returned from a yearlong venture to Texas, with tales of a rich virgin land abundant with fruit and game.

"A land flowing with milk and honey. The Promised Land!" seventy-two-year-old Elder John expounded, standing up before the assembly and quoting scripture. "I've heard the Lord's calling, leading us in that direction!" Elder John was the patriarch of their Predestinarian 'foot washing' Baptist church and when he spoke everyone listened.

"I don't care what they say, I'm not going to Texas," Rachel declared in a muffled voice. "We'll all be killed by those savage Comanche Indians or eaten by wild beasts and I'm not going. I'm staying here with Uncle Joseph and Aunt Martha." When James and his family lived in Arkansas he made several trips into Texas exploring the country for possible homesteading. Rachel had often overheard her father's account of horrifying Comanche Indian raids on settlers.

Six-year-old Cynthia Ann, standing on the opposite side, poked her in the ribs. She was a cute little girl with long, honey yellow hair and sparkling blue eyes but could be a little impish. "Oh!" Rachel grunted, looking down at her cousin's mischievous smile and then to where she was pointing. Furrowing his brow, Elder John glared at Rachel with penetrating eyes. He allowed no disturbance in his church.

Elder John and his wife, Sallie, along with six sons, their families and in-laws, made up about half the congregation. Other members consisted of the Browns, Kennedys, Jordons, Greenwoods, Lagos, Bennetts and Robinsons. Before the church service ended most had agreed to sell their properties and move to Texas.

It took over two months for the families to prepare for the long, extended journey to Texas. Homesteads had to be sold. Wagons, equipment and other goods, necessary for the trip, had to be purchased. Very few items of furniture would be carried. All other furnishings were sold with the house. Only the essentials, such as cooking utensils, bedding, clothing, food, farm tools and seed, could be carried in the wagons. Even then they would be overloaded. Due to the heavily loaded wagons, some families traded their mules for oxen, which were more adapted at pulling strenuous loads through rough terrain and for long distances.

The sun's edge was just showing in the eastern sky as the oxen plodded along, with their heavy burdens, down the wagon road leading to Fort LaMott. It was there all families were to assemble to begin their long journey.

Thirty-five-year-old James Parker had traded two of his best working mules for a team of oxen and a saddle horse. James, a tireless, broad shouldered, man with a tanned face and rough leathery hands, was akin to the rest of the Parker men – brave, tough and wily, willing to risk all for the rich, virgin lands of Texas. A true pioneer.

With his saddle horse and a milk cow tied to the back of the wagon, James hiked alongside the oxen, prodding them occasionally to keep moving at a steady pace.

"Rachel, you can just stop that pouting. It's not going to do you any good," her mother, Patsey, scolded. "We are all going to Texas.

You cannot stay."

Rachel, her mother and one-year-old baby Frances, were riding on the front seat of the wagon, while four-year-old James either trotted along by his father, or rode on one of the oxen.

"I just know we're going to be captured or killed by Indians and I'm scared," Rachel muttered.

"Honey, I know you're afraid but you're being unreasonable. All the Fox, Sac and Delaware Indians have left Illinois and settled west of the Mississippi River."

"That's right. And that's exactly where we're headed – across the Mississippi to St. Louis, Missouri," Rachel said knowingly. "All the Indian tribes in Missouri have joined together and their chief is that fierce Black Hawk. When we leave St. Louis we'll be at their mercy. If we're not captured and made slaves by them, we'll surely be killed by the Comanches when we reach Texas."

"Rachel, I want you to stop this nonsense right now!" Patsey demanded impatiently. "You're worrying over things that will never happen. We are going to Texas."

When I turn fifteen I'm going to marry a man that will take me back to Illinois and Mother can't stop me, Rachel brooded. *Anyway she's been a little on edge about this trip too. I heard her and Papa talking.*

We were leaving the comforts of our home and many of her prized possessions to travel hundreds of miles to a wilderness of unknown perils. This is all Papas' fault, Rachel surmised. He and my uncles and Grandpa are always wanting to move to that 'wonderful rich land flowing with milk and honey'.

Standing up in the wagon Rachel caught a glimpse of Fort La Mott on the horizon. As the oxen rounded a bend in the road a line of wagons came into view, seemingly a mile long. Drawing closer she counted twenty-five ox-driven wagons and hordes of people meandering about.

James directed the oxen in behind the wagon of his newly married daughter, Sarah and her husband Lorenzo Nixon. The wagon train now numbered twenty-six.

Presently Benjamin Parker came riding his mount down the line, stopping at each wagon and speaking to its owner then moving on to the next. Not being married and having a family to take care of, Ben took on the responsibility of wagon master.

"You folks ready?" he asked James.

"As ready as we'll ever be."

"We'll be leaving when I get back to the lead wagon. You have any trouble, just send one of your girls to fetch me," Ben announced before turning and trotting his horse back to the front.

On the morning of the third day after leaving Fort La Mott the wagon train was on an open prairie of rolling hills and valleys that extended from horizon to horizon. By late afternoon the caravan came to rest for the night at the National Road. This was the main wagon road leading to the settlement of Vandilia and on to East St. Louis where they would cross the Mississippi River.

The next morning, at the crack of dawn the wagon train moved on again traveling westward over the National Wagon Road.

Slowed only by crossing rivers and streams, which sometimes took most of the day, the caravan of wagons made good time.

After almost two weeks of slogging over rain soaked roads and prying wagons out of bog holes and creek, they arrived at East St. Louis on the east side of the Mississippi.

Sitting astride her papa's horse Rachel gazed out at the immense body of water. Its vastness was unbelievable. *Where did all that water come from?* She thought. *Where does it go?*

Along the riverbank boats and barges of all sizes were tied up to docks extending out into the water. From these, Negro slaves labored at loading and unloading barrels and crates. Steamboats, laden with goods, moved out into the swift flowing river toward the west side, some pulling barges filled with animals and wagons. Rachel had never seen anything like this. The sight was overwhelming. Far across this massive body of water stood the town of St. Louis, Missouri.

It took two days to ferry the caravan of people, wagons and animals to the west side of the Mississippi. The town of St. Louis was enormous. Buildings lined the road as far as one could see. Hordes of people in wagons, on horses and afoot moved up and down the streets.

The wagon train turned southward following a road to the outskirts of town where they camped along the riverbank. Here they would rest for two days while purchasing supplies for their long journey.

While individual camps were being set up Benjamin dropped by each campsite to inform the families they would all meet together for an evening meal and fellowship to commemorate the crossing of the Mississippi River. Afterwards there would be a time of prayer, asking for guidance and safety as they now would be facing many hardships, traveling hundreds of miles through rough, unsettled territory.

The late evening sun was beginning to sink below the treetops when most folks finished their meal and gathered for prayer. Their long and hazardous pilgrimage to Texas still lay ahead.

The procession of wagons moved slowly along the river road southward, crossing flooded streams that cut through the land before pouring into the great Mississippi. Often their banks were steep and creeks too swift to ford without endangering wagons and livestock, causing the wagon train to detour many miles upstream to a more suitable crossing. Along the way the group passed no dwellings and met few travelers.

In the evenings, when wagons stopped for the night, fires were built for cooking. After a hearty meal everyone bedded down around the wagons without pitching their tents.

Sundays were different. On Saturday evening the wagons came to rest early and tents were set up with the intent of staying until Monday morning. All food preparation for Sunday was made at this time. Sundays were for rest and worship. There would be no work, only daylong services of preaching and singing, breaking of bread, and other Baptist ordinances. Also, the ritual of foot washing was practiced to demonstrate their love for each other.

Over two months had passed since leaving St. Louis, Missouri when the pilgrims pulled their wagons into the town of Natchitoches, Louisiana, clustered along the Red River with numerous stores, shops and dwellings. The town was alive with all manner of people – black, white, French and mulatto, mostly bustling about through the town's market and river docks. Others seemed content just sitting idle in the shade, watching the caravan of twenty-six wagons creep along the river road. After passing the last dwelling the wagons pulled over under a grove of live oak trees skirting the river and stopped for the night.

Leaving Natchitoches the wagon train headed southwest to Nacogdoches, Texas. After crossing into Texas the group continued to wander the immense regions of the state trying to locate suitable land to homestead. During this time the only Indians seen were in the eastern part of Texas near the town of Nacogdoches and they were friendly Cherokee. But Rachel was still determined to go back to Illinois.

At one point the travelers halted at a place called Grimes Prairie where log shelters were built to protect them during the winter. Here, the men scouted out the country for a place to put down roots. The place chosen was east of the large Trinity River, a day's journey from Fort Houston.

* * *

The four men heaved the log up waist high and set it in place on the unfinished wall. Luther Plummer, along with James, Benjamin and Daniel Parker had worked all morning cutting and fitting sixteen-foot logs into walls for a church building. Luther leaned back against the incomplete wall and mopped streams of sweat from his face with a shirtsleeve.

Despite this being the middle of March the warm midday sun and Texas insufferable humidity had sapped the men's early morning energy.

"Come on Luther," James beckoned. "Let's get cleaned up. I think the women are about ready to set the food out."

"I'll be along shortly. Just gon'na sit here and rest a minute." he grunted, hopping up on the four-foot wall.

Poised on the wall Luther stared down at the ground, allowing his thoughts to reflect back over the many months since arriving in Texas. *It seemed they had rambled through this vast wilderness forever before finally settling in a permanent place, east of the Trinity River and about a day's journey from Fort Sam Houston. And now, after building several cabins, there was talk by some of the Parkers, of moving to a more favorable, fertile land west of the Navasota River.*

Almost a year had passed since leaving Illinois. A year of traveling through mostly unsettled country, we seldom stopped for any length of time, always on the move. When would it ever come to an end? When would they finally put down roots and stay?

Almost from his birth in Maryland in 1811 Luther had lived a rugged, unstable life. At an early age his parents died and he was sent to stay with an uncle. When he turned fifteen he left and joined the army to fight Indians. Instead, he was assigned to an army work camp in Canada. Fed up with the army Luther deserted and eventually found his way to Illinois where he met the Parkers. With the promise of free land he set out for Texas with his new extended family.

Now at the age of twenty-three there still seemed to be no permanence – nothing of the family life he envisioned.

"Hey Luther. What'cha thinking about?"

Jolted from his pondering thoughts he glanced up to see James Parker's daughter, Rachel, standing with her hands on her hips, wearing an impish grin and eyeing him with those large blue eyes that seemed to sparkle.

"Uh, oh, nothing," he stammered. "Just thinking." Luther had known Rachel for over two years but never before had he been aware of just how attractive she was. *If she was two years older, I'd see James about doing some courting,* he thought.

"Is that a new dress?"

"Uh-huh. Mother made it for my birthday. I'm fourteen-years-old today," Rachel announced with a smile, showing dimple indented rosy cheeks.

"Well, happy birthday. You've certainly become a very mature young lady."

"You think so? Sarah married Lorenzo Nixon when she was fifteen. I may get married when I'm fifteen – that is if I can find the right man," she teased, giving that mischievous smile again. "Come on. We're going to be late for the noon meal," Rachel coaxed, grabbing Luther's hand and yanking him down from the wall.

And I may just marry you, Mr. Luther Thomas Martin Plummer, she thought.

* * *

The wedding was held under a large arbor constructed near the log church building. Luckily it was a bright sunshiny day and everyone dressed in their finest attire.

Daniel Parker, dressed in his black preaching clothes, looked very staunch as he and Luther stood patiently waiting at the front of the arbor while the attention of the entire assembly was focused on the church door, waiting for the appearance of the bride.

At last Rachel stepped out, hanging to the arm of her father. They strolled leisurely up to the alter where Luther took her by the hand and they knelt in front of Daniel.

Dressed in her sister's beautiful wedding gown with her silky red hair braided and woven into a bun in back, Rachel posed a striking bride – looking so grown up – no longer a fifteen-year-old girl but a mature woman.

Following the ceremony a large wedding feast took place under the arbor. Baskets, laden with all kinds of food, were brought in and set out on split log tables. As the people crowded around, laughing and talking while filling their plates with delicious food, Luther and Rachel ambled around the crowd thanking each one for coming.

By mid-afternoon most folks had drifted back to their homes, leaving only a few scattered around in small groups. One group of men gathered around Luther joshing him about married life.

Over in one corner of the arbor Rachel sat alone on a bench writing in her diary – a gift from her mother.

March 22, 1834

Today I turned fifteen and married Luther Thomas Martin Plummer, who is going to take me back to Illinois. He just doesn't know it yet.

* * *

The Parker clan, along with the other families who traveled with them to Texas, had been living at their present site, on the east side of the Trinity River, for over a year. Cabins had been built, crops planted and some had filed claim to their 4,600-acre homesteads. Their church, called the 'Pilgrim Predestinarian Regular Baptist Church', had been built and Daniel Parker elected as their pastor. A few months after Luther and Rachel were married she became pregnant and on January 16, 1835 their son, James Pratt, was born. By all appearances the group of pioneers was settled. Still, others continued looking for more fertile land to homestead.

During this time James and Silas, along with a few other men set out westward in hopes of finding better land for their new homes.

After crossing the Navasota River they found a rich country lying at the junction of the black land prairie of central Texas and the post oak belt. The virgin forest of oak, ash and walnut along with small meadows and springs of unlimited water made the country ideal for homesteading. The vast acreage of fertile land had everything the Parkers had sought after.

Returning to their homes with a good report of abundant fertile farmland just west of the Navasota River, they were met with some opposition from several families who viewed the move as too dangerous. Hearing of frequent Indian attacks in the central and south regions of Texas, they elected to remain near Fort Houston. Others had already filed their land claims and built their homes. Among these was their church pastor, Daniel Parker.

In the end only nine families loaded their wagons and eagerly pushed on.

At Fort Houston the travelers rested and purchased needed supplies before crossing the Trinity River and embarking on their westward journey through unmarked territory.

In the afternoon of the fifth day, after leaving Fort Houston, they crossed the Navasota River. Moving uphill the party set up camp near a spring-fed creek. Here their long and sometimes challenging journey came to an end. In this land of plenty they would build their homes and plant their fields.

In the late evening Elder John Parker stood in the back of his wagon and called for a time of prayer and thanksgiving. Opening his bible he read aloud:

And the Lord had said unto Abram, get thee out of the country, and from thy kindred, and from thy father's house, unto a land that I will show thee: (Genesis 12:1 KJV)

"Through our obedient faith and courage in following that inner voice of God and pushing on, today we have entered that land," Elder John proclaimed proudly.

The next morning as the Parker men were preparing to cut logs for the construction of housing, five men rode up, three on horseback and two in a wagon. Two of the men, David Faulkenberry and his son Evan, Silas and James had met during their search of land for homesteading. The Faulkenberrys had settled on land just a few miles from there.

"Good morning James," David said, dismounting his horse, "I got word you and your people pulled in here yesterday evening and set up camp. I've brought some neighbors with me to help cut timber for your homes. You know my boy Evan. That old toothless codger sitting on that black horse is Mr. Lunn and the two in the wagon are Silas Bates and Abram Angelin. They all live close by. You still thinking of constructing a stockade around your homes?"

"Yeah. We reckon its' best to build a fort since we're over forty miles from Fort Houston," Silas Parker stated.

"A Fort!" Rachel blurted out. She was standing nearby and overheard the conversation. "Why are you building a fort? Are we going to be attacked by Indians?"

"Never know little lady," Old Man Lunn declared in a raspy voice, letting a wad of tobacco juice slip from his mouth and splatter in the dirt. "Best be safe than sorry. Those Comanche and Kiowa devils are always after horses and will do anything to get um."

I've been warning everyone of this since we left our homes in Illinois, but no one would listen, Rachel brooded. *That's why I'm going back.*

It took over two months to complete the fortress. Its walls of twelve-foot logs, standing upright, with hewn pointed tops, enclosed an area of over one-acre with two-story blockhouses constructed at the northeast and southwest corners. Ten feet by twenty feet log cabins with a fireplace were built against the walls, three on one side and four on the other.

Access to the enclosure was by a large double gate at the northeast end and a small gate at the southwest end.

Built for the purpose of protecting both families living inside the walls and those living in the vicinity from Indian attacks, the fort was impregnable.

In the late spring of 1835 the Parkers moved into their new homes.

At long last, after a two-year trek from Illinois they now were at the end of their journey.

For the next year the Parkers plowed their fields, increased their stock and settled in to a secure life.

* * *

April 1836

"Rachel! Rachel!" she could hear Luther calling her name but it seemed to be in a dream. Rachel opened her eyes and set up. The room was pitch black.

"Get out of bed. We haf'ta leave. Hurry!" Luther said impatiently.

"Wh-What's wrong?" she sputtered, scrambling out from under her quilt and searching for her dress.

"Silas returned from south Texas and said the Mexican army of two-thousand, under General Santa Anna invaded Texas about a month ago and on March 13th his troops wiped out the garrison at the Alamo in San Antonio. See if you can get a fire started and make some coffee. I'm going out to get the mules hitched to the wagon!"

"Wh-Why do we have to leave?" Rachel pleaded. "That's over two-hundred miles from here."

"Because they're now moving eastward across Texas, following the retreating Texas army and driving out all settlers, burning and slaughtering everything in sight," Silas said. "Everyone is urged to flee to Louisiana. Now hurry!"

I always knew something terrible would happen to us in this unsettled wilderness, Rachel thought. *And now it has.*

Rachel heard the cabin door open and shut. In the dim light cast from the fireplace she could see Luther just inside the door, wet from the rain now peppering the roof of their cabin. It was April and there would be rain, rain and more cold rain – miserable weather. She

20

poured Luther a steamy mug of coffee.

"Everyone is getting packed. We'll be leaving just as soon as it's light enough to see," Luther announced. "We'll need to pack all our food, bedding and clothing in a tarp to keep them dry."

By the time they were packed the rain had stopped, leaving an overcast sky in the early morning light.

After dousing the fire, Rachel bundled up her baby boy, James Pratt, who was now sixteen-months old hustled out the door and clambered up into the wagon. Looking around the fort compound she could see others hurriedly loading necessary items into their wagons. The gates to the fort were wide open and all livestock, not being used, was driven out and set free. Everyone rushed to get moving.

For four days and nights it rained incessantly as the caravan of wagons lumbered slowly eastward across muddy-prairies and rain swollen creeks toward the crossing of the Trinity River. On the fifth day they came to a tree-covered knoll overlooking the Trinity bottom where hundreds of people stood watching the waters of the rain swollen Trinity flood the river bottom cutting off all hope of crossing.

For the next four days hordes of people camped near the flooded river waiting for the waters to recede. On the fifth day two men came bounding into camp on mud splattered horses, sliding them to a stop before the large group of people.

"The Mexican forces have been defeated!" they shouted. "Sam Houston and his Texas army victoriously crushed them on the plains of San Jacinto! Santa Anna has been captured! You can all go safely home."

With joyful hearts the Parkers returned to the fort, gathered their livestock, plowed their fields and resumed a life of peaceful existence.

Captors and Captives

May 19, 1836

All day and into the night the Indians and their captives rode northwestward across large prairies and through tree-lined creeks, never stopping. The captives were so bruised and battered that each step of the horse sent waves of searing pain through their bodies. The two children, Cynthia Ann and John, so raw and weary from riding could scarcely hold onto their captors. Baby James, who rode with a squaw, could be heard whimpering for his mother, only to be clouted with a fist.

The feet of Rachel and Elizabeth were drawn tightly against the horse's sides by thongs tied under its' belly. Had it not been for the plaited rawhide cords restraining them, they would have fallen to the ground. With wrists tied together they meshed their fingers into the horse's mane. Even then it took all their concentration to keep balanced.

Rachel's dress hung in tatters and her back was ridged with purple welts. With the constant jolting and jarring of her insides, she wondered if her unborn child would ever survive. Mile after weary mile they rode. The trek to nowhere seemed endless.

Waves of horror crawled through Rachel's mind. The nightmarish slaughter played over and over. The screams of agony mingled with unearthly yells of savage Indians echoed and penetrated her thoughts.

Will they kill us? Rachel thought, struggling with consuming fear, absent of any hope. She tried to pray but even prayer would not come. Why had God allowed such a massacre and abuse of His innocent children? Why pray?

On and on flowed the stream of horses carrying both captors and captives. The only sounds to be heard were the rhythmical trod of horses' hooves, the whimpering of John, Cynthia Ann and baby James and the occasional howl of wolves.

Finally, around midnight, the Indians with their exhausted prisoners came to a stop near the Brazos River. Here John and Cynthia Ann were dumped to the ground and their feet and hands tied.

With the rawhide thongs untied Rachel slid from her mount and tried rubbing life into her blood starved feet, but was knocked to the ground by a squaw. Urine stung her chafed legs as terror caused her to lose control.

Dragging Rachel and Elizabeth Kellogg close together the Indians threw them face down and tied their ankles and wrists so tight that blood welled up from beneath the cruel cords. To keep the captives from turning over they drew their feet and hands together with a plaited thong. With the two prisoners tied, the squaws commenced beating them about the head until they were almost smothered in their own blood. As the men passed, they kicked their cringing bodies.

In her half-conscious state Rachel could hear the sobs of her bruised and suffering baby boy, crying out in dreadful distress. "Mother! Mother! I want my mother!" Each time the cry was hushed by a blow.

The love Rachel felt for her dear child and the scorching anguish that filled her soul seemed more than she could bear. "Oh, how much can my heart endure?" she groaned in agony. "Dear Lord give me strength. Only you know my suffering."

When the Comanche and Kiowa Indians halted around midnight with their prisoners, they staked their horses and pitched camp around a huge fire. Erecting a pole, with scalps of their unfortunate victims dangling from the top, they commenced dancing and leaping around it, shouting and chanting. With dreadful demonic yells, that would terrify the bravest heart, they leaped into the air, contorting their bodies in a re-enactment of the murders they had committed. While this was taking place one of the young warriors squatted in front of Rachel showing her a small bottle filled with white powder, pilfered from the raid. The bottles label said 'Pulverized Arsenic'. Rachel gave no hint to its purpose. Satisfied it was some type of paint the young Indian and three others painted their faces and bodies after dissolving it in their saliva. Within an hour lamenting squaws carried their dead bodies away for burial. This did not hinder the fiendish ceremonial ritual, which continued until the wee hours of morning.

"Rachel! Rachel!" Elizabeth called in a weak voice. "Are you OK?"

"Water!" she uttered piteously through parched lips. "Oh! I need w-a-a – oomph-gasp!" Two Indian women standing guard jumped with their feet upon Rachel and Elizabeth, bashing their chests into the ground, leaving them gasping for breath, and choking on the mold dust of the forest. They never spoke to each other again.

During the hours before daybreak Rachel could hear the children helplessly begging for water.

The next morning, with captives again secured to the backs of horses, the Indians turned northward, traveling from morning until night through a varied country of small prairies skirted with timbers and many springs.

Even as she suffered with excruciating pain from the inhumane treatment received from her merciless captors, Rachel could not help but admire the beauty of this diversified country. It was a land abounding in rich grassland, streams and timber of every description.

The evening of the fifth day, after leaving Fort Parker, the party came upon a vast grassy plain. On the distant horizon Rachel could see a tree line that appeared to be running northeasterly. Upon reaching this woodland the Indians followed a buffalo trail as it meandered through the deep forest until arriving at the Wichita River. On the opposite side columns of smoke from many campfires could be seen, rising above the treetops.

As the sun hung low in the western sky, the prisoner's horses followed obediently with the band of Indians as their ponies sloshed across the stream and up its high bank to a small Indian encampment.

That night, for the first time in almost a week, Rachel, Elizabeth, John and Cynthia were given their first taste of decent food, which was some type of meat stew. Up until then they were given only scant amounts of water and scraps of meat. Afterwards they were again separated and their hands rebound behind their backs.

During the time since their abduction, the captives were kept separated, sometimes not seeing each other for days. When they did, they were not allowed to speak and would be brutally beaten if they did.

Unable to rest lying on the ground, Rachel shifted her bruised, aching body to a sitting position and using her feet inched herself to a tree to lean against. In this position she was able to release some of the pressure of the plaited thongs that bound her hands, cutting flesh so deep she felt at times her swollen hands would never be useable again. Her bruised and battered face was swollen to the point that one eye was completely closed.

Occasionally Rachel stole a glance at Elizabeth lying curled on her side. The pitiful sight of her poor aunt's marred body made her heart ache with distress. Her hair, now in tangles, was matted with dried mud and blood. There didn't seem to be an inch on her body that was not cut or scratched. Only her periodic jerking indicated she was still alive.

Rachel could hear her child's heart-wrenching wails, continually calling "Mother", but the Indians would not let her see him nor speak to him. Finally her bonds were removed and a squaw brought little James Pratt to his mother to nurse.

"My Baby! My Baby!" Rachel cried. Too weak to stand she held out her arms toward him.

As soon as he saw his mother he rushed into open arms where she embraced her darling boy's trembling, frail, mutilated body with love and sorrow.

"Thank you Lord," Rachel muttered, tenderly caressing her son, thinking they had given him back to her. "Thank you my Lord for softening the hearts of my captors."

When the old squaw saw that the child had been weaned she snatched him out of Rachel's arms.

"Mother! Mother! Mother!" little James screamed, reaching out his hands toward his mother as he was carried away.

"No! No!" Rachel cried desperately while being restrained by two Indian women who thrust her face down on the ground and retied her fetters. "Please don't take my baby!" she pleaded. With all hope lost, Rachel buried her face in the soft dirt and leaves and sobbed. "Oh Father protect my little boy." In her heart she knew this would be the last time she would see her precious James Pratt, but would one day meet again in that heavenly place prepared by her Lord and Savior.

All that night into the early hours of morning the captives were kept awake by the ear piercing shrieks, screams, and howls of their sadistic abductors and other tribes of Indians as they conducted their hideous barbarous dances. The monotonous chanting and pounding of drums never ceased.

* * *

The stinging bite of a whip across Rachel's face and arms jolted her awake and into a sitting position. Her hands, still tied behind her back, had become numb and the throbbing pain was almost unbearable. A large squaw with a leather quirt said something and motioned for Rachel to get up. When she tried to stand, only to fall, she was whacked with the quirt. Grabbing Rachel by her red hair the woman jerked her to her feet.

Two other Indian women with whips had forced Elizabeth to stand. They were then pushed over where several squaws were cooking over hot coals and forced to sit down. Moments later Cynthia Ann and John were brought in along with two Mexican women captives, and sat down across from them. No one spoke, not even Cynthia or John, for fear of being beaten. Not hearing James Pratt, Rachel feared he might be dead.

Looking around at everyone's cut and battered faces almost made Rachel sick. Poor little John's lips were so puffed out, he probably couldn't talk if he wanted to. Cynthia's pretty blue eyes were almost swollen shut. Seeing how badly they had been beaten, tears mounted in Rachel's eyes.

Later, after eating their bowl of mush, they were yanked to their feet by Indian braves and pushed into an arena circled by several Indian tribes. Their dress indicated they were not all Comanche. It was then that Rachel realized they were to be traded like Negro slaves at a slave auction.

Elizabeth Kellogg was purchased by the Kitchawas; Cynthia Ann and John by a band of Comanches; and Rachel went to another band of Comanches. They were then separated, never to see each other again.

That night Rachel lay on the cool ground, tethered by both feet and hands, praying. Praying for the safety of her two cousins and aunt. Praying for her beloved darling son. Praying that the Lord would give her strength and courage to endure.

"Oh precious Lord", she moaned. "I know I should forgive and pray for my enemies, but I cannot. Please forgive my unfaithfulness. I can only pray that You, My Father, grant them a merciful heart."

With her eyes closed she tried to block out the horror of her surroundings and let her mind wander back to the blissful security of a life she would never see again. With these peaceful thoughts she drifted off to sleep.

Aftermath of Fort Park Attack
May 19, 1836

Moments before Fort Parker was attacked by hundreds of Comanche and Kiowa Indians, G. E. Dwight, his wife and two children, his mother-in-law, Mrs. Frost and her two children rushed out the back gate toward the Navasota River where he planned to conceal them in the river bottom thicket before returning.

At the same time Sarah, James Parker's daughter and Lorenzo Nixon's wife, fled toward the cornfield to warn the men working there. Following close behind her was James's wife, Patsey, her two children and her two grandchildren. They soon met up with James, James Wilson, Lorenzo and Luther Plummer hurrying from the field after hearing the piercing cry of Sarah.

Upon hearing the fort was under attack, James sent Luther to alarm the neighbors, and told Lorenzo to proceed on toward the fort, he would catch up after hiding the women and children in the forest.

"Patsey! Take that trail to the river! Hurry!" James shouted, snatching up two of the youngest children in his arms. "Run, Sarah!" he hollered. "I'm right behind you!"

* * *

James Parker

Reaching the Navasota River James hoisted the two children on his shoulders and waded across the waist deep water with Patsey and

James Wilson right on his tail. He then went back for Sarah and the other two children. Hiding them where they would be safe, he re-crossed the river and set out for the fort.

A few yards from the river he met up with G. E. Dwight, his wife and two children, and Mrs. Frost and her two children. All had escaped the fort unharmed. Mrs. Frost was sobbing uncontrollably, tormented with the thought that her husband, Samuel and her son, Robert, had been killed in the raid.

Wading back across the river the group located Patsey, Sarah and the children. Following the tree-lined thicket of the Navasota River southward, they hoped to find other survivors of the attack.

"James! James!" a soft muffled voice called desperately.

"Wh-where! Dwight did you hear someone call me?" James sputtered.

"Yeah. It came from that tangled thicket of vines."

The group could hear breaking of underbrush but could not see anyone. The heavy growth of brambles was so thick that sunshine could scarcely penetrate through its' curtain of briers. Moments later a woman and two children crawled out of the snagging brush.

"Lucy Parker, is that you?" James asked.

"Uh-huh" she gasped, pulling a thorny brier from her flesh. "Are the Indians gone? I - I was afraid they would find me and the children" she mumbled tearfully.

"We don't know. Lucy, are you alright? We heard John and Cynthia Ann were taken captive. We'll do our best to get your children back," James declared.

Lucy was so distraught she could not speak, but held tightly to her children, uttering her husband's name over and over. She seemed to hold no doubt her husband, Silas, had been killed in the attack.

"Lucy, have you seen Lorenzo?" Sarah asked, hopefully.

"Yes," she mumbled in a trembling voice, tears trailing down her face. "The last I saw of him was when he and David Faulkenberry hid me in this brushy line of timber. Said they were going to look for the group of men with Luther."

"Sarah, I'm sure Lorenzo is OK," Dwight assured. "When I saw him earlier he was searching for others who fled the fort. He's probably with some of our neighboring families."

"It's getting late. I think it best we stay right here until dark. When the moon comes up we'll make our way to the nearest settlement," James stated. "I'm sure that's where the party with David Faulkenberry and Luther will be going."

The group with James now numbered eighteen, of which twelve were children from one year old to twelve.

Barefoot and destitute of food, with no means of obtaining any, the small company of families huddled together in the trackless wilderness of the Navasota River bottom inhabited only by venomous reptiles and ravenous beasts. Despair seized every heart as they fearfully expected to fall prey to the savage Indians at any given moment.

As darkness gathered in the forest James thought of slipping into the fort with the hope of finding food and possibly some sign of what had happened to other families living in and near the fort. When he mentioned this to his companions they all agreed he should not go. They would rather risk starving than for him to leave, fearing he may fall into the hands of the enemy. In that event, they would perish in the wilderness, as all were ignorant to the direction in reaching a settlement.

For the next hour the group set on the ground, talking very little. James had told them sound traveled a long distance on a still, clear night and the enemy may hear them.

At first it was just a dim glow peeking through the timber. Then slowly, the first rim of a full moon surfaced over the treetops and began its ascent into the night sky.

"It's time to go," James said, shouldering one of his children and leading the other.

With other adults following his example, they began trudging through the thickly entangled briers and underbrush, following the Navasota River southward.

* * *

Granny Parker

At the onset of the Indian Raid Granny Parker was knocked to the ground, stabbed multiple times and left for dead. But, in the late evening when the fort lay quiet, she began to regain consciousness.

In the distance Granny could hear someone moaning, then realized the groans resonated deep within herself. Slowly the dark curtain lifted, bringing with it a surge of petrifying fear. Then came pain, excruciating pain that racked her body with every heartbeat.

She lay face down in the dirt while oozing blood, from knife wounds, seeped into the dry earth. A few feet away lay the body of her husband, stripped of clothing and riddled with arrows. His scalp ripped from his head, leaving only raw meat and bone.

Granny opened her eyes. "Oh John! What have they done to you!" she wailed, raising her throbbing head.

Where are the others, she wondered*? Were they taken by those hideous people? Oh dear Lord, I must hide before they come back.*

The late evening sun was now creeping below the west fort wall. It would soon be dark. With darkness came visions of roving wild beasts of the forest and bloodthirsty Indians, lurking behind shadows of the night.

"I've got to find the others," Granny gasped. Bringing her knees up she painfully, in slow motion, raised her body to a crawling position. "Oh my God," she sobbed, seeing the lifeless bodies of Samuel and Robert Frost and her son Silas. "Merciful Lord, where were your protecting hands?"

Daylight was slipping away as Granny, on hands and knees, inched her way along the forest trail leading her to the cabin of Seth Bates, a neighbor who lived outside the fort. In the forest twilight a vision of something or someone moving up the pathway in her direction caused her to stop. Grasping a tree she managed to pull herself to a stand, then hid behind its' large trunk.

* * *

Luther Plummer

Upon hearing the fort was besieged by hundreds of Indians, Luther Plummer and the other two men working in the cornfield threw down their hoes and hurried toward the fort. They soon met up with James's wife who confirmed the Indian attack.

Hearing her words of distress Luther raced off to warn the four neighboring families who lived in cabins not far from the fort. With seven or eight armed men they could rush to the aid of the people in the fort.

Out of breath and gasping for air Luther covered the mile distance to the Faulkenberry's cabin in less than ten minutes. Finding David and his son, Evan, working their field, he quickly blurted out that Fort Parker was being raided by Indians, as they spoke.

David sent his son to the Bates' cabin to fetch Seth and his son Silas, then set out, with his rifle, for the fort. Luther, though winded, left for the Anglin's cabin to get Elisha and his son Abram.

The brilliant sun was set in the sky when the party of men assembled together about 500 yards from the fort. The group consisted of Luther Plummer, Evan Faulkenberry, Seth and Silas Bates, Elisha and Abram Anglin, and Old Man Lunn. All armed with a rifle except Luther who had only a butcher knife.

Skirting through the timber the group reached a point where the fort could be seen in full view. Seeing hundreds of mounted Indians scattered around the fort whooping and shrieking the men slipped back into the forest to plan their attack.

"What are you men planning on doing?" a voice stated abruptly from behind the seven men, causing them to turn with their guns at ready.

"Faulkenberry! Where have you been? Have you seen any of my family? Have you seen Rachel?" Luther asked desperately.

"Just rescued Lucy Parker, her two babies and Lorenzo. They were fleeing from mounted Indians about a half mile from the fort," David said catching his breath. "The Indians saw me raise my rifle and backed off. Lorenzo took Lucy and her babies to hide in the thicket. Lucy's other two children, John and Cynthia were taken captive. She thought Rachel and your son were taken too. I don't know how many people got out of the fort but those that didn't I'm sure are either dead or captured."

"Let's get to the fort and kill as many as we can!" Luther blurted out in a tight voice.

"Luther you don't even have a weapon except that knife in your hand. They'll have you speared and riddled with arrows before you can get within fifty feet of them," David protested. "Fellows if we go up there now we'll all be killed, leaving our families in this wilderness to fend for themselves. Those devils are going to be looking for the ones who escaped out of the fort. We best go search for them and make sure they're out of harms way."

"David's right," Old Man Lunn declared. "You men best take care of your loved ones still alive."

"My family has been taken captive and I'm going after them," Luther said bitterly.

"With a knife? Luther you'll be killed," David argued.

"I'm gon'na follow them until they stop and bed down for the night. Then sneak in and release the prisoners. They won't be expecting me."

"You don't even have a horse. Here, at least take my rifle."

"Don't need one," Luther stated confidently and walked away.

With that said the other men set out for the bottom land thicket along the Navasota River to search for their families.

* * *

Abram and Evan

The last rays of a setting sun were dipping below the treetops when Abram Anglin and Evan Faulkenberry slung their shot pouches over their shoulders and picked up their rifles.

"Where you boys think you're going?" Abram's father questioned, frowning. The group of men had located most of their families and were holding up in the river bottom until daylight.

"We're going to ease back to the fort to see what's going on. There may be some survivors."

"I don't think that's a good idea. That's just what those redskins are hoping we'll do. There's going to be a full moon tonight and they'd pick you off one by one."

"Evan and I will be OK Pa. We'll not take any chances."

"Alright. But you boys head for the thickets if you see any sign of Indians."

33

Dusk had faded into darkness as Abram and Evan picked their way through the tangled thickets and emerged out on a dim wagon road near Seth Anglin's cabin. Just as they passed the cabin Evan caught his breath and grasped Abram's arm, bringing them both to a halt.

"What is it?" Abram whispered.

"I – I don't know," Evan stammered in a muffled voice, "I thought I saw something moving up ahead."

As the boys stood, with their rifles drawn, letting their eyes search through the dim haze of darkness, a vague shadowy form, dressed in white with long white hair streaming down its back, issued forth.

"It's a ghost!" Abram uttered frantically backing up with his gun at ready.

"Look Abram! It's beckoning for us to come on!"

As the boys drew near, the figure murmured, "Help me," and fell to the ground.

"It's Granny Parker," Evan exclaimed. "She's hurt bad. Granny! It's me and Abram. We're going to help you. Abram, get something we can carry her on!"

In minutes Abram was back from the cabin with a sheet. Placing her on the sheet they carried her out of the wagon road to a safe spot in the timber.

"Granny, are the Indians still here? Are there any other survivors?" Abram asked.

"I think the Indians are gone," Granny mumbled. "My John is dead and so are others."

"Are you going to be alright while Evan and I check the fort for anyone else alive?"

"I think so. I want you boys to get my money for me. You'll find $106.00 in silver buried under a bush beside my cabin."

The first rim of a full moon had surfaced over the treetops and began slowly ascending into the night sky as Abram and Evan cautiously approached the fort. Inside they could not find a single individual alive or hear a human sound. All they heard was a dog barking in the distance and a few cows lowing outside the fort.

Finding no one in the fort they retrieved Granny's money and returned to where they had hid her in the forest. On their way back to the river bottom with Granny they came upon Lorenzo Nixon who helped in toting her in the sheet.

It took over an hour of searching through the dull-lit timber and brush before the three men, with their seriously injured burden, located the group anxiously waiting their return.

"Is that Granny Parker?" David asked. "Where did you boys find her? Is she dead?"

"No sir," Abram answered. "But she's hurt pretty bad. We found her near Seth's cabin." Laying Granny on the ground in their midst the women tried as best they could, under the light of a pale blue moon, to clean her wounds.

"I'm going to find Sarah and my children," Lorenzo announced.

"You better wait till morning Lorenzo. You may get lost in this bottom thicket," David warned.

"No. I'm going now."

"Then I'm going with you. You don't even have a rifle."

"No. I'd rather go by myself," Lorenzo insisted. "I'll be alright." With that he painstakingly made his way through the tangled forest.

* * *

Mrs. Duty

A black vale now covered the land bringing with it a fearful silence as Mrs. Duty, Rachel's grandmother, lay hovered in the dark forest, listening for the slightest sound. Only the chirping of a bird could be heard. The throbbing in her chest, where she had been wounded, was becoming unbearable.

When she first saw the multitude of fierce Indians bounding for the fort on their fast horses Mrs. Duty had scrambled out the back gate and dashed for the bottomland. She had managed to flee only to the edge of the timber before being caught by two painted horsemen, stabbed and left for dead.

With searing pain shooting through her body she managed to stifle a mournful cry and kept her eyes closed until she could no longer hear the diminishing sound of horses' hooves. Weakly, she crawled into the forest where she fainted.

It was late evening when Mrs. Duty opened her eyes and looked around. She tried to move but the sharp, stabbing pain in her chest and side were too excruciating and she fell back on the ground.

In a daze she watched the full moon gradually creep up over the trees, casting out the darkness with its dim blue light. Within minutes scary shadows, made by overhanging limbs, appeared on the ground.

She had been lying in the same position for many hours, when she heard the cracking of twigs underfoot and the rustling of leaves. Raising her head the image of a human creature emerged from the shadows into the pale light of the moon. With eyes squinted tightly closed, Mrs. Duty dropped her head back to the ground.

"Oh Lord, they're going to kill me," she moaned.

Several seconds passed then came the snap of a twig close to her head. She squeezed her eyes tighter, waiting for the final blow. A strong hand reached down and turned her over.

"Mrs. Duty! Mrs. Duty! Can you hear me? This is Lorenzo Nixon."

Her only answer was a groan. Stripped of every vestige of clothing, she lay mangled and bleeding on the cool ground, while her life-blood ebbed from her wound. She had been stabbed in the right breast with a large knife, which did not enter the chest, but passed off, near her ribs.

Lorenzo tried to pick her up but she fainted in his arms. His only means of reviving her was by bringing water to her in his shoe. Finally, after great exertion, he succeeded in getting her to a neighbor's empty cabin. After covering her with a sheet, he left to go for help.

The gray light of morning was filtering through the trees when Lorenzo arrived back to the company of people he had left earlier.

"Lorenzo! Where have you been all night?" Seth Bates asked. "We thought you'd run into a party of Indians."

"Didn't see Indians but I found Mrs. Duty. She's been stabbed and is in pretty bad shape," Lorenzo said anxiously. "I carried her to an old vacant cabin but I'll need help in getting her here."

"If one of you men will stay with the women some of us will go help fetch Mrs. Duty," Elisha Anglin spoke up.

A decision was quickly made that Mr. Lunn would stay and the other three men would return to the cabin with Lorenzo.

After dressing her wounds the party carried Mrs. Duty back to their hiding place in the bottom.

The two boys, who had returned with Granny were now back from their second trip, bringing with them six horses and saddles, cornmeal, honey and bacon. For fear the Indians might return, the five dead men at the fort were left lying where they fell.

With the aide of the horses and provisions, the group with Lorenzo and David Faulkenberry set out eastward to a settlement near Fort Houston, sixty miles away. They did not know what had become of James Parker and those with him.

* * *

James Parker

Even with the pale blue shadowy light of a full moon the progress was very slow for the families in the company of James Parker making their way southward through the brier infested river bottom. Most were barefooted and many of the children had nothing on but a shirt. In some places the brambles were so thick that the briers tore the legs and arms of the children until blood trickled down to their feet. Their sufferings were heart-rending.

The group traveled until about 3:00 in the morning. The moon had now gone down leaving them in darkness that covered the forest. Being fatigued and hungry they lay down in the grass and slept until dawn.

Sunlight was filtering through the trees when the party again resumed their weary journey, leaving the river bottom in order to avoid the briers. Seeing the tracks of Indians and horses in the high land, they thought it necessary to return to the brambles of the river bottom.

James had made the decision to take his group to Tinning's settlement. There, they would be able to obtain food and shelter, and the safety in numbers. The settlement was seventy to ninety miles away, depending on the route they would be compelled to travel.

Their journey would take them through an unknown, hostile, wilderness of many unforeseen perils, and there would be little or no food.

By the fifth day of trudging through, what at times seemed to be an impregnable jungle of tangled undergrowth, the women and children's feet and legs were so lacerated and swollen they could hardly walk. Overcome with fatigue and hunger they could go no farther.

It was then agreed among the men, that James would continue on and bring back help. Those that stayed prayed that God, in his bountiful mercy, would provide James the strength and perseverance, in the trying hours of his journey to the settlement.

In the early afternoon of May 25th, six days after the raid on Fort Parker, James stumbled into the Tinning settlement. The first house he came to was owned by Captain Carter who promptly offered James all the aide in his power.

Soon six horses were saddled and James, accompanied by Captain Carter and Jeremiah Courteny, set out to rescue the little company of survivors. Just before dark they met up with them along the bank of the Navasota. Placing the women and children on horses they arrived back at the settlement around midnight.

Here they received kind attention and relief from the sympathetic people of the community.

On May 27th, word was received that the company with David Faulkenberry had arrived safely at the settlement of Fort Houston. Lorenzo Nixon, Sarah's husband, being one of those.

Luther Plummer, who left to search for his wife and child, wandered through the country afoot for many days before finally making his way to the Tinning's settlement.

Comanche Village
May & June 1836

In that hazy moment, between being asleep and awake, came a feeling she could not escape. Was someone watching, or only a dream? The throbbing pain shooting through her arms and shoulders said NO.

She lay curled in a fetal position on the hard earth. Hands, completely absent of any feeling, bound tightly behind her. Sleep had come only in fitful waves of horrifying dreams. Rachel opened her eyes.

In the pale dawn light she could see lean brown legs standing so near the moccasin encased feet almost touched her face. Cringing, she squeezed her eyes shut and waited, praying it would go away.

Hearing the cracking sound of campfires, people moving around, and voices she could not understand, Rachel cautiously opened her eyes. The feet had not moved. Almost unwillingly her eyes were drawn upward, past a breechclout and a bare upper body, to a high cheek-boned face still covered in a painted mask, now cracked and peeling, giving him a blotchy encrusted satanic look. Fixed with an uncompromising gaze he leered at her with dark penetrating eyes, encircled with black paint.

Seeing she was awake, he crouched down so near Rachel was overcome by his foul breath. She winced when he reached out and touched her. *What was he about to do?* Tears began to gather in her eyes.

"Ah-ha!" a strong angry voice shouted.

Rachel looked up to see an older warrior scowling with blazing eyes at the young buck bent over her. He quickly stood up and with a nasty sneer on his face jerked a scalping knife from the leather sheath strapped to his thigh.

He's going to kill me! she thought. *Oh Precious Lord, deliver my soul.* Muffling a sob, she held her breath and waited.

Using his foot, he pushed her face down on the ground and proceeded to hack off her beautiful long red hair, leaving it cropped off just below her ears. He then cut the rawhide cords that bound her hands and snatched her up by her docked hair. With his knife held in a threatening position to her throat Rachel knew instinctively that if she made any trouble at all she would be killed as casually as crushing a fly.

The pressure in her bladder was almost painful. How much longer could she hold it. How could she tell him of her basic needs?

With numb hands she made flourishing gestures of the need to go relieve herself. He pointed to the ground. Hiding, as best she could in the tail of her frayed skirt, she squatted at his feet, shamefully.

Tethered by the wrists with a horsehair rope, Rachel was led to the campfire where several women labored in cooking and getting ready for another day of traveling, a pattern that took place every day. *Where were they going?*

Through the gray light of morning Rachel could see many fires along the riverbank and Indians meandering about. Their numbers had increased during the night and still more were trickling in, driving or riding their stolen horses. Some had Mexican captives. The herd of stolen horses, picketed by young boys in a clearing, had grown into hundreds. *This must be one of their gathering places after a raid,* Rachel thought.

After receiving a few meager scraps of near raw meat Rachel was tied to a tree while preparations were made to leave.

When the young Comanche returned with saddled horses Rachel noticed that his black hair, plaited in two long braids, was interlaced with her own red hair. Rachel indicated her need for water. He handed her a skin pouch. She had barely wet her lips before he snatched it away. *Oh how she longed for a few more drops.*

Mounting the horse Rachel's hands were again bound by leather fetters, this time to the saddle horn. Thankfully her feet were not tied together under the horse, as they had been for the past week, which had left her legs, thighs and buttocks bruised and raw.

All day they rode, camping at night near a river or stream. The land being very rich in game furnished an abundance of meat. As the raiders ate they would occasionally toss sizzling pieces of roasted venison to Rachel, then laughed at the sight of her struggling to eat the small bits after falling in the dirt. Constant hunger ate at her insides, keeping her weak and disoriented.

All day the ever-increasing band of Comanches, along with their captives and hundreds of stolen horses, traveled steadily across a seemingly endless flat plain of buffalo grass. With no covering from the scorching sun, Rachel's fair skin became inflamed with agonizing blisters. Landmarks became nonexistent, wiping out all hope of escape.

It was mid-afternoon when the mass of people and horses arrived at the low, sandy land bottom of the Red River. The river, bordered on both sides by a broad expansion of tall grass and scattered trees, was wide but very shallow.

Seeing wisps of smoke rising into the sky beyond the trees lining the opposite side, Rachel assumed they would cross. But instead, the party came to a halt in a group of trees along the banks of a small stream that emptied into the river. While the stolen horses grazed along the river, Indian warriors made preparations for their triumphal entry into the village on the far side.

Using handfuls of dry grass the Indians brushed their horses until shining and embellished the animals head and body with red and yellow stripes and circles. With this completed the warriors began to preen themselves. With a porcupine-quill comb they dressed their hair, plaiting in extra hair taken from captive women and adorning it with beads and feathers. Arrayed in full regalia of painted faces and ornamental deer skin leggings they were now ready to make their gay, imposing entrance into the village.

With loud whoops and yells announcing their approach to the village, the Indians, captives and stolen horses bolted across the Red River and up the opposite bank to be met by cheering young boys on horseback.

The entire Indian village poured out to greet them amid shouts, dancing in wild excitement. The warriors, trailed by their ill-gotten captives and horses, pranced through the irregular settlement of wigwams and stick huts, accompanied by an enthusiastic escort of old men, women and children.

Riding through the village Rachel noticed that all children, even those appearing to be seven or eight years old, wore little or no clothing, and was surprised at seeing a number of children of light complexion. She later learned they were the product of white women slaves or white traders who exchanged goods for the affections of an Indian woman.

Rachel was terror-stricken of the frightful women and children surrounding her who yanked her from the horse and began to inflict heavy blows upon her. They were finally dispersed by a young Indian buck who appeared to be a chief. Clasping her arm in an iron tight grip he began to drag her toward a hut where a fat old Indian man sat lazily in its' shade. With a few sharp words the Chief deposited Rachel on the ground and left.

For several minutes the ugly old man looked down at Rachel with a nasty sneering scowl then gestured to the woman and young girl standing in the doorway to take her inside.

The aged woman, who appeared to be somewhat older than the man, yanked Rachel to her feet and shoved her into the dwelling. She was a short-bodied, homely-looking woman who wore a constant sour expression across her leathered face. The young girl, who seemed to be thirteen or fourteen years old, pursed her lips and followed them inside where the two women cut off Rachel's wrist bands and stripped her of what remained of her filthy garments. She was then dressed in a well-worn deerskin dress.

Exhausted and barely able to walk, due to raw saddle sores between her legs and bottom, she was immediately put to work gathering firewood and fetching water. Rachel now realized she had been given to the old Indian man and his family. As a servant she must reverence the old man, his wife and daughter as her master and was forced to do their every bidding.

The man called his wife *Wa'ipu* (woman) and his daughter *Taabe* (sun). They called the old man *Tenahpu*. Rachel, who was called

Narairo (slave), was instructed to call the old man *Narumi* (master).

As a slave Rachel was required to carry in firewood, fetch water, cook all meals during the day and mind horses at night.

Though overworked, with little rest and sparse amounts of food, Rachel counted it a blessing to be claimed as property of the old man. As a servant to his family she seldom came under abuse of others and he would rebuke any young brave coming near her.

Early on the third morning of arrival at the Red River the whole Indian village seemed to be in commotion. Children scampered around laughing and screaming, dogs barking, squaws scrambling hither and thither pulling down tepee poles and rolling up their buffalo hide covers. Cooking utensils and other items were packed and placed on travois poles attached to horses. Small children, placed in buffalo skin sacks, hung from saddles or their mother's back.

Rachel, working under the instruction of Taabe and her mother in packing their tent and other belongings, was amazed at how quickly the entire village became dismantled and made ready for traveling.

While young boys on ponies took charge of the horse herd, the women and children either rode or led the packhorses.

All being ready, the multitude of people and animals, moved out in one long motion, northward. Out in front of this procession were the Indian braves, riding together upon good mounts, leaving the women and children to trudge along with the burdened packhorses.

Stretching out before them, to the horizon, lay a rolling plain of prairie grass.

Near the end of this long line of travelers, amid the whirling dust of those before her, Rachel struggled along leading a packhorse. Tired and bewildered she wondered of their destination in this strange far-off land which appeared to reach out forever.

* * *

In the early morning on the third day of their journey the Wichita Mountains began to rise up like a dim shadow on the horizon. Sometime around mid-afternoon the band of Indians and captives ascended a high rise in the immense grassland. Here the group had a panoramic view of the mountains foothills.

Excited shouts of '*Kuutsuu! Kuutsuu*!' spread up and down the line of people who watched as twenty or more warriors bolted their mounts toward the mountain valley.

From her view Rachel could see only a large dark shadowy mass drifting across the lower grassland of the mountain range.

"*Kuutsuu?*" Rachel said to her young mistress.

Taabe turned and pointed at the buffalo horns and hide tied to the travois poles.

"Buffalo! Those are buffalo?" Rachel declared turning again to see the mass of movement, which numbered in the hundreds. Rachel had seen buffalo hides and even pictures of buffalo but never a real live buffalo, nor in such great numbers.

The hunters approached the herd from downwind. There were a hundred times more than the men could kill or the women to skin and dress. They directed their efforts against a specific bunch grazing in a pocket, which hid them from the others.

While the women, children and old men waited on the knoll until the killing was over, the hunters advanced in a semicircle on the small herd with their horses in a walk. When the animals began to run they were forced into a circle and easily killed by the skilled marksmen.

With the buffalo now on the ground bleeding and dying the women rushed down to the killing field to butcher and skin the carcasses.

Rachel thought it strange how none of the men, young or old, made any effort to help, just as they offered no assistance when moving the village. She soon was to learn females, young and old did all the labor.

That evening, with the Indian camp set up along a mountain-fed stream, Rachel experienced her first lesson in the grueling and laborious task of dressing buffalo skins. While her two mistresses sat on a rock giving instructions Rachel toiled at the drudging chore for many long hours.

Spreading the hide on the ground Rachel scraped all flesh and fat from one side and the thick hair from the other. The skin was then put in a large hole in the ground, filled with water, to soak and be trampled upon for several hours making it pliable. After soaking for a few days the skin would be vigorously rubbed with a mixture of animal fat, brains and liver to soften the hide. Later it would be smoked over a fire to give it a light tan color.

When darkness fell over the village at night Rachel's chores were not complete. Tired and weary, with painful festering sores from physical abuse and a broken spirit, she must now keep watch over her master's horses.

After staying several days at this place the Comanche's left in the coolness of early morning following the flowing stream as it wound its' way through a valley in the mountains. By mid-afternoon the procession emerged out into an immense valley of prairies, which intersected, with the green graceful slopes of tree covered mountains. Hundreds of acres of yellow, purple, white and blue wildflowers flourished across the grassy plain, bathing the earth's surface in an array of color.

Extending down, along a mountain slope and out into the valley stood a forest of hardwood trees of many varieties. It was here, on the banks of a river, a great encampment could be seen.

The first glimpse Rachel had of the Comanche camp was unforgettable. Clusters of buffalo-hide tepees were strung along the river for several miles. Making the village look even more populous than it really was. Hundreds of horses grazed nearby. Hordes of people stood watching as they drew near the encampment. Entering the village her captors dismounted and greeted their friends. Family members set up tents near one another.

The warriors were met with shouts of joy as children rushed out to see what had been brought back from their long trip.

Men, women, children and dogs, all curious to get a look at her, surrounded Rachel. Once she was on the ground Comanche children flocked around, all wanting to touch her red hair. This continued until the old mistress sent them away, putting Rachel to work assembling their dwelling. She was hopeful the people would stay here for more than their usual two or three days. After so many weeks of continuous traveling, over hundreds of miles, her exhausted body was so weak she could scarcely move.

That night, lying under a crude tent listening to the lonely howling sound of coyotes, her thoughts turned to home, family and friends so very far away. Greatly discouraged she longed to be back among civilized humans. But, escape was near impossible. *Even if she did manage to escape where would she go? The plains stretched away on all sides, vast and featureless. There would be wolves and hunger and thirst and slow death. There would be no place to run – no hiding place.*

For now she had no apprehensions in regard to her personal safety so long as she remained an obedient slave, fulfilling all duties imposed on her by her master.

Rachel thought of her mother and father and all her siblings and friends. *Were they killed – and Luther her husband. Was he alive? Was he looking for her? And if he found her – what then? She would never be clean? The putrid smell of the Comanche's beaver-oiled bodies would linger on her for the rest of her life. It could not be removed. Luther would never want to touch her. She hated to touch herself. There would always be murmurs and whispers as she passed among civilized people.*

Tears began to sting Rachel's eyes. She yearned to hear Luther's voice and feel his arms hold her safe. The knowledge that she was totally alone and helpless in a brutal and hostile world overwhelmed her and she wept. Then silently she began reciting Bible verses.

Colorado Rocky Mountains
July – October 1836

The travois poles, laden with piles of buffalo robes and other possessions, bounced and clattered over the rocky ground. The column of people and horses winding their way along the river stretched for more than a mile.

A month had passed since leaving the beautiful valleys and mountains of the Wichita. Moving in a northwest direction, never staying more than two days in one place, the large band of Comanche Indians had crossed the Canadian River, the Cimarron River and was now on the Arkansas River following its path westward.

Rachel riding near the end with a few Mexican captives choked on the dust blowing in her face. Her lips and the skin of her hands and legs were now cracked and bleeding. *How much longer would they travel like this?*

Occasionally she would feel her baby move inside and be reminded of her son, James Pratt, and she would grieve, praying for his safety.

Day after day, the band of nomadic people drifted across the treeless plains. Gradually the Rocky Mountains began to rise up as a thin line on the horizon. Within a few days the towering rugged peaks of the blue mountain range began to take shape.

Reaching the foothills, the travelers continued to follow the river route as it twisted and turned through the valleys and canyons of the mountains.

At times the treacherous rocky path seemed to disappear as high canyon walls pressed in on the rushing river, but always opening out into a grassy plateau where game was abundant.

For two weeks the large band of Comanches trekked higher and higher. Finally the towering canyon walls gave way to a large mesa of high grass and scattered trees extending in every direction three to eight miles reaching the base of tree covered mountains. This was the headwater of the Arkansas River.

In the heart of this savanna rose a treeless tableland some twenty to thirty feet higher than the surrounding meadows. Snaking around its northern base flowed the Arkansas River. Here the Comanche people set up their extended village.

This luscious grassland plain, abundant in elk, deer, bear and buffalo, served as a paradise for large communities of roving Indians, who depended mostly on wild game for food.

Late in the evening when long mountain shadows covered the earth and the coolness of the day began its drop to near freezing Rachel sat watching her master's horses while laboring to complete the rubbing-down of an unfinished buffalo skin. Tearfully she pondered her hopeless situation. She was now over seven months pregnant. A thousand miles from family or friends, in the heart of the Rocky Mountains where no white man had ever been. No possibility of ever being rescued. Exhausted and weak, she had now deteriorated to a sickly specimen of what she once was. Rachel questioned if the Lord Himself had abandoned her.

The Comanches camped at the headwaters of the Arkansas River for two weeks killing game for their meat and pelts. Leaving this place they followed a well-used route southward over Poncha Pass and down into the San Luis Valley, a grassland plain of springs, wetlands and an abundance of game and other wildlife. This age-old valley between two mountain ranges expanded outward twenty to sixty miles and extended south for over seventy miles to the Rio Grande River.

On the third day of their journey the travelers set up their village near springs of bubbling hot water. Large pits were dug and the Indian men bathed in the hot mineral waters seeking healing of old battle wounds received while engaging raids and wars against the Apache and other Indian tribes.

Longing to bathe her bruised and battered body in one of these pools, Rachel asked permission to do so from her old mistress, Wa'ipu. After more than four months with the Comanche she had acquired the ability to understand and speak, haltingly, in their language.

"No!" the old woman shouted with a scowl on her weathered face. "It is reserved for our warriors."

Taabe, who stood nearby, never missing an opportunity in taunting Rachel, hissed with a sneer. "You are a slave. A white slave. Do you think we would allow your defiled body to tarnish the waters our brave warriors wash in? I would kill you first."

With a heavy heart Rachel slipped away to gather dry chips of buffalo dung for a cooking fire.

"Lord, please smother the hatred I feel for these cruel, callous-hearted people, who lack any form of human compassion."

For a moment Rachel's thoughts returned to the world she was taken from and remembered the inhuman treatment of black slaves by some of her own race. She could now empathize, to some degree, the plight of the Negro slaves.

On leaving the place of bubbling springs the band of Comanches set out for a mountain range looming up on the western horizon. It was there, in the foothills of these mountains they intersected with the 'Old Spanish Trail', which meandered southward to the Rio Grande River.

In reaching the Rio Grande, around the first of September, a light snow could be seen blanketing the high mountain peaks. Here in the valley the early mornings hovered at freezing.

Their camp, now consisting of close to a hundred tepees, stretched out a great distance along the rushing river.

The following morning the Comanches were visited by a caravan of traders from the Spanish-Pueblo Indian settlement downstream. They brought carts laden with corn, beans, potatoes, squash and even pottery, knives and trinkets to barter for furs and horses. These people used the river to irrigate the fertile valley, producing an abundance of vegetables.

This was Rachel's first encounter with a friendly, more civilized people since being taken captive. Even their clothing of colored fabric gave signs of a more kind hearted culture.

Knowing Rachel may see these traders as a means of escape, her master had her hands and feet bound and placed her in a tepee.

Two days later the camp was dismantled and moved westward up the Rio Grande through a mountain pass, which followed the river as it snaked around gigantic crags of rocks.

On the second day they trudged out of the pass and looked out on a treeless grassland plain of beautiful rolling hills and meadows with many branches of the river flowing through it. Here rested the headwaters of the mighty Rio Grande River. This scenic savanna seemed to continue in all directions as far as the eye could see, joining with the distant mountains whose topmost peaks showed white from early winter snow.

While the procession made their way along an age-old path, Rachel could see herds of elk and deer feeding in the still green meadows. Occasionally a group of big horn sheep scampered away into the mountains.

What a peaceful and beautiful place, she thought. *This must be where they intent to settle.* Being now heavy with her unborn baby, Rachel's hopes soared.

In the weeks to come Rachel suffered more from cold than she had ever suffered in her life. Seldom did she have anything to put on her feet and very little covering for her body.

Many times it was necessary for her to take the buffalo skins with her when minding the horses at night in order to complete the assigned number. Often her feet would be almost frozen but she dared not complain.

During the months since her capture Rachel grew to understand not only the Comanche language but also many of the customs. In their culture, raiding and plundering their enemies and taking captives, were not regarded as acts of cruelty, but deeds of honor. It elevated their importance and exalted them above others.

In many respects they were akin to the heartless slave owners of Missouri and other southern states who felt no guilt or shame in the ill treatment of other human beings.

Wrapped in a buffalo robe against the frigid north wind, while watching her master's horses, Rachel pondered her unfortunate fate. It was during these times that she found a ray of reassurance reciting the words of the Psalmist and felt the comfort of the Heavenly Father's loving hands.

Though I walk through the valley of the shadow of death, I will fear no evil: for thou art with me: thy rod and thy staff they comfort me.

Thou preparest a table before me in the presence of mine enemies: thou anointest my head with oil: my cup runneth over.

Surely goodness and mercy shall follow me all the days of my life: and I will dwell in the house of the Lord forever. Psalm 23: 4-5 KJV

* * *

Lying under the heavy scratchy buffalo robe Rachel bit her lip and listened to the angry voices outside the lodge. A group of enraged Indian men were arguing with her master and two mistresses. From what she was able to understand it was pertaining to her and her unborn child. *What horrible thing awaited her? Would she be killed? Were they going to take or possible kill her baby?*

Rachel cowered under the robe, too frightened to move. She needed to relieve her bladder, as she had so many times that day, but dared not go outside. How much longer could she hold it? The extreme pressure caused her to leak on her skirt.

Had her water broke? She wondered. *Was the baby coming?*

Moments later the dispute ended and the old Indian and the two hard-faced mistresses opened the skin flap door and stepped in, bringing a gust of cold wind and snow. Without a word spoken Wa'ipu and Taabe grabbed Rachel and thrust her out the door where she was met with the bitter cold winds of October. Even with a buffalo robe wrapped around her Rachel's teeth began to chatter and her body shivered.

Was she being pushed outside to freeze to death? "Let go of me!" Rachel shouted, trying desperately to pull away. "What are you going to do to me? Don't hurt my baby!"

The two women led Rachel to a small tent, a short distance away from other lodges. Inside lay a few sticks of firewood, a skin of water, a fur blanket and a scant amount of deer jerky.

Wa'ipu handed Rachel a knife and ordered her to dig a small hole in the ground for the afterbirth. When complete she took back her knife and handed Rachel a sharp stone with which to cut the umbilical cord. With instructions for her to stay until after the child was born, the two women left.

All day and into the night Rachel huddled near the small fire inside her chilly tent, waiting expectantly for her child to move. She listened to the mourning of the frigid wind outside the tent and let her thoughts wander back to the home she was taken from – yearning for her mother's comforting hand as she birthed her second child – a warm bed – a consoling voice.

But she was alone with no one to help. *What would happen to her – to her baby? Would they kill the child?* Tormented with the certainty that they would, Rachel wept in agony.

In that painful hour, just as the morning light began to peek through the small seams of the tent, a baby boy was born. Though weak and exhausted, Rachel found strength to clutch her crying, bloody child in her hands and cut the cord. Afterwards she lay resting on the soft furs with her tiny boy, bundled in a rabbit pelt beside her. Tears of happiness rolled down her face while she watched her infant child nurse at her breast.

For the next few weeks Rachel found the Indians were not as hostile as she had feared. But, when the child was about five weeks old Tenahpu began to complain, repeatedly saying the infant was interfering with her work, and the child's constant crying was becoming very annoying. From that day on Rachel feared for her darling son's life.

Rachel tried reasoning with the old warrior, telling him that due to receiving only a meager amount of food her milk was not sufficient for her baby, causing him to cry for more.

The old Indian ignored her, saying the child was too much trouble and a burden to him and his family.

Rachel begged her mistress to tell her how to save her child but the old squaw turned a deaf ear to her pleading.

On a clear cold November morning Rachel set at the entrance to her master's lodge nursing her baby boy, while watching clots of snow melting in the unshaded places. A gentle breeze, warmed by the morning's sun, breathed through the doorway and created a feeling of early spring.

Glancing up she noticed five large Indian bucks stalking toward her, their hard bronzed faces were contoured into a beastly scowl. Rachel's heart sank and her whole body began to shake with fear, almost to the point of convulsion. She knew their intention.

Rachel wanted to flee but it was too late. "NO! NO!" she shrieked, falling to the ground and covering her precious child, as the five warriors stepped into the tent.

One of the savages reached down and wrenched the child from his mother's bosom. Rachel frantically struggled in vain to free her baby, but the other Indians held her back.

"Don't hurt my baby! Don't—" her scream was cut short by a blow to the head. Falling to her knees Rachel threw back her head and wailed.

The Indian holding the baby grasped it by the throat and with an iron-clasped grip choked it until, by all appearances, he was dead. The devilish braves then took the infant by the feet and hurled him into the air, laughing hellishly each time he hit the hard earth.

Rachel, still kneeling on the ground sobbed uncontrollably. All effort to save the child was fruitless.

When the Indians were certain there was no life remaining in the little boy's body, they tossed him back into his mother's lap.

Overwhelmed with grief Rachel washed her darling infant's bruised and bloody face with a fountain of tears.

After some time he began to breathe again, showing some trace of lingering life. When the heartless men noticed it had recovered they again tore the child from his mother's embrace, knocking her to the ground.

The Indians then tied a plaited rope around the child's neck and drew his naked body through prickly pears several times before tying the rope to the saddle of a mounted horse, dragging him until he was not only dead but his innocent little body literally torn to pieces.

Rachel knelt, horrified at the dreadful scene playing out before her. With her hands covering her ears to block out the demonic laughter, she rocked back and forth while her mournful cry filled the air. "My God, My God, Why has thou forsaken me? Why would a God, who said He loved me, rip out my heart and take my children?"

One of the Comanche men took the mutilated infant by the legs and threw it into Rachel's lap.

Tenahpu, who stood by watching the diabolical act with an expressionless face, stalked over and kicked Rachel to halt her anguishing wails. With a stern voice, absent of any feeling, she was told to get rid of the child and start taking down the tepee. The encampment was moving to another location.

With pleading eyes Rachel implored her master to allow time to bury her little boy. After much tearful begging the old stone-faced Indian relented and permitted the heartsick mother to bury her child.

With her hands and a stick Rachel dug a hole in the earth and buried her son, giving praise to the Lord for softening the hearts of her captors in giving her the time to perform this last service to the lifeless remains of her infant son. She then knelt at the grave and gazed with joy on the resting place of her now happy boy – she then prayed:

"Holy Father, I can now say with King David, 'You cannot come to me, but I must go to you'. Even now Lord I rejoice that it has passed from sufferings and sorrows of this world. I am fully confident, believing and solely relying on the righteousness of my Lord and Savior Christ Jesus, that my happy baby is now with its' kindred spirits in that eternal world of joy." *

"Father, my broken heart now fails to forgive my enemies as you have taught us. So, I ask Lord, as Jesus did, 'forgive them for they know not what they do'. And cover me Lord with your Holy Spirit that my callous heart may heal and I can say, with in my transformed soul, 'I forgive'."

*Rachel Plummer Narrative (paraphrased) #21

54

The Comanche Indian

The Comanche name was most likely derived from the Spanish interpretation of the Ute name, 'Kohmahts', meaning 'those who fight against us'. They once lived at the edge of the Rocky Mountains near the upper reaches of the Platte River in eastern Wyoming, along with the Shoshone or Snake People (Ute). Making their homes of bark in the forest of the mountain valleys, they lived by hunting, fishing, digging roots and occasionally killing a buffalo. They were known as 'hunters and gatherers'.

Sometime during the 1600's the Comanches separated from the Shoshone and migrated to the Great Plains of eastern Colorado and western Kansas. By the 1700's they had crossed the Arkansas River and established themselves on the large plains of Oklahoma, Texas and New Mexico. Here they no longer hunted buffalo on foot but pursued them from their fast, sturdy horses left by the Spaniards. With their swift horses they were superior in battle, defending their lands against the native people (Apache and Kiowa) eventually driving them out. They then had the freedom of roaming over their vast territory, making frequent raids on European, Spanish and Native American settlements.

The Comanche now dominated western Oklahoma, northeastern New Mexico and the Texas plains. Their fearful raids into Mexico, seeking horses, weapons, goods and women slaves, became a yearly event.

When it came to horses the Comanche Indians were the finest horsemen on the continent. Everyone rode horses starting in childhood. By age four or five both boys and girls were accomplished riders. Boys, at the age of fifteen or sixteen, were experts in shooting game with bow and arrows from their fast moving mounts and were now ready to join raiding parties.

On their swift mustang horses they swept down on unsuspecting Texas settlers, brutally massacring the men and kidnapping women and children – then fleeing any pursuer.

The Comanche Indians were a cooper-colored race having thin lips, straight black hair and dark brown or black eyes. The men were of medium stature with a solid built well-proportioned erect frame. The women appeared to be prematurely aged due to their heavy workload and nomadic life.

The Comanche men took great pride in their personal appearance, especially their hair, which they wore long and rarely cut. After brushing and greasing, they parted it in the center from forehead to neck, then braided their hair in two long braids tied with leather thongs.

The women did not let their hair grow long but kept it short and parted in the middle. Like the men they painted their scalp along the parting with a colorful paint. It was not unusual for both men and women to adorn themselves with various ear ornaments, dangling from one or both pierce ears.

Accept during the winter, Comanche men wore only a breechclout, which was a long piece of buckskin brought up between the legs and looped over and under their belt at the front and back. Sometimes loose-fitting leggings, extending down to their moccasins, were worn. Women wore long deerskin dresses. In the winter warm buffalo robes and knee-high buffalo hide boots were worn by both men and women. Unless it was cold weather, the very young children went naked.

They referred to themselves as the *Nememe*, meaning 'our people' or *Nermeruch*, meaning 'people of the people'.

Being a nomadic people they seldom stayed more than three or four days in one place, unless it was very cold weather, then only staying until the weather changed.

The women did all the work in packing for the move. They took down the pole and buffalo skin lodges, bundled and strapped the skins and other wares to horse pulled travois then set out for the next camp. With the exception of going on raids and killing the meat women did all drudgery tasks of setting up lodges, cleaning and cooking the meat, dressing skins, watching the horses, etc. The men danced almost every night, during which the women waited on their every need. They were no more than servants and were looked upon and treated as such.

When a pregnant woman was ready to deliver her child she would find a convenient place in the tent to lie down upon, then remove the grass and everything else from the surface of the ground. Upon this spot she would pass her hour. When the child was born she covered it with a blanket, went to the nearest stream, bathed herself and the baby and returned to her business the same day, as though nothing had happened. This would be true whether at home or on a journey.

Dancing was a part of the Comanche worship, as was torturing prisoners. They worshiped such things as a pet crow or a deer skin painted with the sun and moon. The band Rachel lived with worshiped an eagle's wing. They also paid homage to a large lump of platinum located on the waters of the Brazos River. Each year they would bring offerings of beads, shells and periwinkles to the place. These things were kept as sacredly as the Holy Scriptures.

The Comanche Indians believed in a Great Spirit, creator and ruler over all, though they had no official name or pantheon for a god. They believed in the resurrection of the body, and future rewards and punishments. But, the white people considered them savages as they did not understand nor accept their form of worship.

The Indians saw themselves as only one element in a work, which nothing was without a spirit. When the Indian sang and praised the sun, moon and wind the white people considered this idol worshiping and condemned them as lost souls, not knowing the Great Spirit is at work in everything – the sun, moon, trees, wind, mountains, etc. Sometimes the Indian people approached the Spirit through these things. They considered their faith much stronger than the white people who called them pagans.

Daily devotion to the unseen Spirit was as necessary to the Indian as daily food. In the course of daily activities he may pause many times in an attitude of worship. To him there was no need to set aside one day as a Holy day since all days belong to God. The Comanches were a practical people who laughed at the religious ceremonies of other humans.

The Comanche regarded fighting as a noble pursuit and went to war seeking glory and goods, especially horses. Also, seeking to avenge friends or family killed in battle. They were determined to hold their hunting grounds of the south plains by driving out all Mexican and American settlers.

Warfare and raids were a part of life. All men became warriors and braves. To distinguish oneself in battle was revered. To die young in combat was glorious. Scalps were trophies to be proudly displayed on shields or on the shaft of their lance. Comanches were always ready for warfare. They were fierce and courageous, yet they sought no mercy if captured. Never surrendered – fought till death.

To the Comanche Indian a captive was merely a slave and a commodity, and was treated as such from the moment they were captured, until their death.

As white settlers moved onto the southern plains, infringing on Indian Territory and disrupting their way of life, the Comanches launched a series of raids and attacks, fiercely resisting the westward movement.

To the white man the Comanches were the embodiment of the 'Wild Indian'. In brutal retaliation, American soldiers and Texas Rangers slaughtered countless women, children and warriors. Even going so far as attacking Indian camps after a peace treaty had been signed, wiping out entire villages of innocent people.

The world of the Indian Nations seemed hopelessly lost to the incursions of the white Americans. It was clear to the Comanches the United States wished to annihilate the Indian race of people.

There was a legend and a prophesy among the Comanches which held that innumerable moons ago all the land from horizon to horizon was inhabited by a rich and powerful white race of people. Their large populous cities were protected by fortifications crowning the mountain summits. A people who excelled over every nation in all manner of crafts and warfare, ruling over the land with a high and haughty hand. They put the Indians to the sword, driving them from their homes and occupying the valleys and mountains in which the red man had dwelt from the beginning of time. At the height of their power, when they were proud and lifted up, breathing out inequity upon the Indian nations, the Great Spirit swept down with fire purging them from the face of the earth, leaving only crumbling remnants of their mighty cities and fortresses.

In like manner, the day would come when the Great Spirit, in his justice, would sweep from existence the boastful and arrogant pale face, who forced the Indians from their lands, despoiling them of their inheritance.

The Indians were confident that, as certain as the rivers flowed downward to the salt sea, and the sun rose each morning, the red man would once again be restored to the land of their fathers.

The Indian people were content to let things remain as the Great Spirit made it. But, the white man would seek to change the mighty rivers of the land if they did not suit him. To the people of the Indian nation, accursed was the race that seized upon the land. Let the white race perish,

We did not think of the great open plains, the beautiful rolling hills and winding streams and tangled growth, as "wild". Only to the white man was nature a "wilderness" and only to him was the land "infected" with "wild" animals and "savage" people. To us it was tame. Earth was bountiful and we were surrounded with the blessings of the Great Mystery. Not until the hairy man from the east came with brutal frenzy heaping injustices upon us and the families we love was it "wild" for us. When the very animals of the forest began fleeing from his approach, then it was that for us, the "Wild West" began.
—*Chief Luther Standing Bear of the Ogalala band of Sioux*

A Nomadic People
November 1836 – March 1837

"Get up off the ground and get to work," Wa'ipu commanded in a sharp tongue. "Take our lodge down. We are moving."

We're always moving, Rachel thought as she knelt by the small grave. *Every few days they moved. Sometimes every day. Can't they stay in one place?*

Rachel stood up and brushed the dirt from her deer skin dress. The fountain of tears she had shed were now dry, leaving only grief. Turning from the grave of her baby boy she walked heavily toward their tent.

"Why must you people move so often?" Rachel blurted out to her mistress. "White people don't move every day."

Wa'ipu looked at her scornfully. "White people do not know how to live. They cut down all the trees for lodges and let their horses eat the grass until there is nothing left of mother earth but bare ground. Then, they walk around like animals, stepping into their own dung. They call us 'heathens'? My people would never live like that. Our people travel to beautiful places to live where there are clear streams and an abundance of game to eat. We can enjoy these places and return to them later to enjoy again."

Squaws were now busy taking down the tepees and rolling up the buffalo skins to be packed on the travois' along with fur robes, cooking utensils, and other goods. Men and boys never helped with the laborsome operation of disassembling the village. Each day she learned more and more of the Indian ways – somethings Rachel would never understand..

This was an exciting time for the Comanche people. They always seemed to be the happiest when mounted and on the move.

When all was ready Rachel raced back and fell upon her child's grave, crying out in anguish. "Lord! Surely you know my sufferings. Why must I suffer like this? What grave sin have I committed against you? My punishment is too great. Oh Dear Jesus help me sustain this cross I must endure."

Oh! Will my dear Saviour, by his grace, keep me through life's short journey, and bring me to dwell with my happy children in the sweet realms of endless bliss, where I shall meet the whole family of Heaven – those whose names are recorded in the Lamb's Book of Life." *

The procession of people rode out three and four abreast, old men, women and children first and captives last. The warriors, rode apart, some behind, some to the sides and some ahead. Dressed in their very finest they set astride their war ponies while eagle feathers that garnished the tips of their lances, fluttered in the wind.

Rachel wanted to take flight on one of the fast horses, and flee from these pitiless people. But, any attempt to get away would result in the severest of penalties, probably death. Even if she successfully escaped she would most assuredly perish in the mountains. The Comanche's watchful eyes were always upon her. Many times she had carefully planned and contemplated her exit only to realize her freedom could only be found in a dream. There was no way out.

Staying alive was all that mattered. It was a waste to think of yesterday or tomorrow. Each morning Rachel awoke longing to be back in civilization with friends and loved ones, only to find herself under a tent, surrounded by a savage tribe – downcast and lonely.

Rachel was tortured continually with an unrelenting memory of her two little children – one in the hands of a cruel people, the other in a lonely lost grave. This, along with daily physical abuse suffered at the hands of her captors, left Rachel's life in little else than unadulterated misery. Still there was the faint hope her family would find and rescue her out from under this bondage of savage slavery.

Each night, when she covered her ears against the pounding of drums and chanting voices, Rachel would cry out "Oh God of

Heaven, only you know why and how it is, that I am still alive. Father have mercy on you child."

* Rachel Plummer Narrative #21

* * *

The Comanche Indians followed a trail that wound between snow covered hills, rising until it crested at the top of a pass. In the distance, jagged white peaks stood like ancient towering walls against the clear blue sky. Far below the wide valley opened into grassy meadows surrounded by green forest. Rushing waterfalls spilled over canyon walls, resting in crystal clear natural lakes before journeying to the rushing rivers. The valley spread eastward toward tree-lined hills and soon gave way to an ocean of prairie, spreading away flat and featureless to nowhere.

As the procession followed a well-worn path downward Rachel could not help but to admire the grandeur and breathtaking beauty of this rugged terrain.

In the early afternoon the band of Indians halted in a pleasant valley protected by mountains where spring weather seemed to have lingered under its' shelter. Here they set up camp.

Rachel was put to work immediately setting up the tepee and cooking a meal for her overriding master and his dominating family.

Later, in the afternoon, when the air turned crisp and the evening sun began splashing slanted rays across the cliffs, Rachel sat on a large boulder working a buffalo skin while overseeing her master's horses. Taabe, who sat beside her watching, felt it would be beneath her to help in the preparation of the buffalo robe when she had a servant to do the work.

"Is it true, what I overheard, that there are hairy beasts in those mountains that have the features of a human, and walk erect?" Rachel asked Taabe.

"Yes. They are called Man-Tiger and are taller than any man. They have hands with long claws that can easily tear a buffalo to pieces. That is why in the mountains, we never separate. No warrior hunts alone."

"Have you ever seen one?"

"No. And I do not want to," Taabe declared firmly. "Some of the older warriors have and they say there is a type of human, no more than three feet tall, living in mountain caves where Man-Tigers are found. The Man-Tigers are aware of the little people and will destroy anything that attempts to harm them."

"I wonder if we will ever see one," Rachel pondered in a quiet voice.

"You better hope not," Taabe warned. "They may kill you. There are other beasts in these mountains more ferocious than the Man-Tigers. The grizzly bears are the size of buffalo and will attack both man and beast. Sometimes a party of our braves will kill a silver white bear. They are very fat and make delicious food. There is also a very large vicious white wolf, capable of killing a buffalo. He too is feared by our people. You must be very watchful of these animals while in the mountains."

After Taabe returned to the village Rachel mulled over in her mind the things she had said. Had she not overheard other stories of those creatures and actually seen a white wolf she estimated to exceed three hundred pounds, Rachel would have thought Taabe was only trying to frighten her into never trying to escape.

For the next four months the Comanche tribe traveled through diversified country along the foothills of the mountains, moving every two or three days. Their village was usually set up near a stream in wide uncluttered valleys. Other times near canyon walls where water percolated out of deep pools, or upon vast prairies, level as the surface of a lake. But, always with the clear outline of the Rocky Mountains in view whose snow covered peaks loomed upward into the sky like a giant fortress around a king's castle. A place of harsh towering beauty.

Prairies were abundant with animals, most of which Rachel had never seen. There were prairie dogs, about the size of a rabbit, loudly barking before scurrying into their ground burrows; prairie fox, no larger than a very small dog with short legs, but very fast; large white rabbits, which created a very tasty meal; large herds of antelope; a great variety of wolves; and innumerable buffalo, whose flesh being the most delicious of all animals. Rachel had often seen the plains covered with these magnificent beasts.

It was during these months on the prairie that Rachel was astonished to discover a large lake of water. Although they traveled directly toward it, they never seemed to be any closer. It always appeared to be no more than forty or fifty steps away. She had never seen a lake or pond any plainer, and it seemed to even have waves. Her thirst was excessive and she panted for a drop of water, but could never get any closer.

Rachel soon came to the conclusion it must be a water-gas forming a mirage. She had once read of such phenomenons, which were common to large deserts and prairies.

She often saw large herds of buffalo feeding in these places. They appeared as though wading in water, their wakes looking as distinct as in real water.

Once the party came upon a salt plain. The salt resembled dirty snow, so light it could be blown by the wind into knee deep drifts. Here they crossed the immense salt lakes having the likeness of a muddy, milky ice.

By March of 1837 the band of Indians was in the vicinity of an abrupt range of the Rocky Mountains that embraces an enormous track of country extending from the headwaters of the Missouri River southwesterly beyond the headwaters of the Rio Grande and north to the Columbia River and headwaters of the Platte River. Some, so incredibly high and perpendicular it was impossible to ascend them. With majestic sharp peaks, these mountains resembled steeples of a church, towering into the sky. In the mountain valleys it could be spring or summer and white winter on top. In these valleys grew wild flax which yielded lint, out of which ropes were made by the Indians.

Many times, from these high pinnacles, Rachel would look out over the country, seeing mountains beyond mountains until they were lost in the misty air, and knew she was lost forever.

Rachel had now been with the Comanche Indians eleven months, seemingly a lifetime of unrelenting toil and abuse. Eleven months since hearing one word of English or feeling the warmth of a comforting embrace or a loving smile. Gone were Rachel's fair and youthful rosy cheeks, cheerful smile and the luster of her long, silky red hair.

Brutal labor with little or no protection from the harsh frigid temperatures of the mountains, blistering heat of the plains, and scant amounts of food, had reduced her strong and vigorous body to a bruised, sickly skeleton. No longer the beautiful seventeen-year-old mother, but a stoop shouldered, wrinkle skinned woman, with a weathered face framed by thick, dirty cropped hair. Blue eyes that once seemed to sparkle now set in deep sockets tired and empty. Yet, having the faintest hope of being released, she never gave up.

Around the middle of March 1837 the band of Indians were again at the headwaters of the Arkansas River. Here they set up their tents among a large assembly of Comanche tribes whose numbers were endless. Their encampments, standing as close together as possible, extended for miles. On a high elevation, in the midst of this vast gathering of lodges, the redskin chiefs held a general war council.

Having been with the Indians all these months Rachel had become very fluent in their language and decided to take every opportunity to listen to the war council proceedings, although it was forbidden for a squaw to be present. Several times she was caught and subjected to harsh abuse, which she submitted to cheerfully, then persevered in listening in on their sessions, which lasted seven days.

During this time the council determined they would invade Texas. It was agreed that those tribes who raised corn would cultivate the farms of the Texas people, and the prairie Indians would have control of the prairies, each party defending the other. It was further decided, after having taken Texas and killed or driven out all the inhabitants, a good supply of corn would be raised, before attacking Mexico. Confident of being joined by a large number of Mexicans who were dissatisfied with their government, they would take possession of Mexico then attack the United States. Too long had the white man driven the Indians from east to west and would even drive them further. It was now time for the tide to turn and the white man driven from their country.

Almost every nation of Indians was represented at this council and all agreed to the plan set before them. One thing was left unsettled, when to attack. Some tribes said spring of 1838, others said spring of 1839. This matter was finally left to the Northern Indians who would communicate to all tribal chiefs.

The week of the war council was now over and the immense

bands of would-be invaders dismantled their shelters and departed to their own section of country.

Before all the tribes had moved on an Indian from one of the bands caught Rachel by herself and stated that he was '*a Beadie*' and lived near the San Jacinto River in Texas. He said his tribe was determined to make servants of the white people. Then he cursed her in English. These were the first English words Rachel had heard since being taken captive.

These few crude remarks, which were never a part of Rachel's spoken vocabulary, brought a fountain of painful grief to her suffering heart. A longing to see, once again, her loving family. There were times Rachel considered death as a blessing. Still she held on to a glimmering ray of hope and faith that God in His infinite wisdom would decide her deliverance.

The Search for Rachel
June 1836 – October 1837

Using a borrowed rocking chair Patsey Parker sat in the shade of a tree, just outside the cabin door, rocking her feverish one-year-old daughter Martha. Two other children, eight-year-old James and five-year-old Frances, lay a few feet away on pallets of old torn quilts. They both suffered from a high fever caused by small pink spots, with gray-white centers, lining the cheeks of their mouth. Patsey could now see a pink rash breaking out on their foreheads that would soon cover their entire bodies.

Measles, generally a childhood disease and highly contagious, spread through families and communities at an alarming rate. There was no cure, but if a patient was kept comfortable and well-nourished it would run its course in a matter of a few weeks. Most adults were immune, if having had the disease in their youth.

After escaping the attack on Fort Parker and making their way through the thickets along the Navasota River to the Tinning's Settlement, James Parker then moved his family farther southward to a more populated settlement near Henry Fanthorp Inn and Post Office located on the 'Old La Bahia Road' in Grimes County.

Having no money and no means of obtaining even necessities, he sought the help of friends who assisted him in acquiring part of a house in which another family lived. It was only one small room with a dirt floor, but met their need for shelter. Soon neighbors began to bring food and other essentials.

With his family now taken care of, James began making plans to return to Fort Parker in hopes of finding the route taken by the Indians with his daughter, grandson and other captives. Just as he completed arrangements for starting back to the fort his whole family came down with the measles.

"I'll not be leaving for the fort with my family sick," James announced firmly to his wife. He had just returned with a bucket of cool water from the nearby spring and was lingering in the shade watching Patsey caress her sickly child while moving to and fro in her chair. "You've been coughing and sneezing all morning. Clear symptoms of coming down with the measles. Never had them before, have you?"

Patsey stopped rocking and peered at her husband through squinted, red-watery eyes that seemed to be sensitive to the mid-day sunlight filtering through the leaves. "The children and I will be fine. I want my Rachel and grandson back. You go find them. I don't care how long it takes. Sarah and Lorenzo are here now to help me out with the children."

James shook his head in exasperation. "Woman you're not in good health and now you're sick with the fever."

"I don't care. I want you to find Rachel," Patsey urged in a pleading voice.

The next morning James, accompanied by thirteen men, set out for Fort Parker, almost one hundred miles through mostly unsettled territory. The company arrived at the fort on June 19th, exactly one month from the time of the Indian siege. They found the fort walls and houses still standing, but all crops had been destroyed and almost all their horses and cattle had either been stolen or killed. Not a single article of household furniture remained intact.

For the next three days the group gathered the scattered bones of James' father and two brothers, and those of Frost and his son Robert (their flesh having been devoured by wild animals). Placing their remains in a roughly made box they buried it among a grove of oak trees located on a small knoll about a mile from the fort.

Finding no trace as to the direction the Indians had taken with their captives, the group of men decided to return to the settlement with as many livestock as could be found.

Arriving back at the settlement James was confronted with the sad news, from Dr. Adams, that his wife was near death and there was nothing more he could do for her. Hearing this, James rushed to his cabin. Upon entering the door he was horror-stricken. His wife and child lay on a pallet of straw, their bodies literally diminished to skin and bones, having the appearance of corpse rather than a living being.

"Patsey! Patsey!" James uttered desperately. "Wake up. I'm back."

Moaning, Patsey gazed up at her husband with ghastly blank eyes, showing no recognition. She appeared to be devoid of any reasoning or any pain.

"Oh my Lord in Heaven," James groaned. "Have mercy on my poor wife and baby."

In agonizing suspense James and his daughter, Sarah, watched over the sick mother and baby day and night, applying medicine he received from Dr. Adams. During this time they continually lifted up anguishing prayers, to their Heavenly Father, for healing.

On the seventh day, father and daughter rejoiced when Patsey set up and began nursing little Martha, responding to them in reasonable conversation. By the second week she and the baby had recovered enough that the two older children, who had recuperated from the measles and were staying with neighbors, were able to return home.

Soon after his wife and child had recovered, James decided to move his family fifty miles farther east from Indian country to a cabin owned by Jessy Parker near the settlement of Huntsville in Montgomery County*. At this time his family consisted of his wife Patsey, their three children, James Wilson, Frances and Martha, and their oldest daughter Sarah and her husband Lorenzo. Also, Rachel's husband Luther, stayed with them when not searching for his wife and baby.

In the early morning of July 1, 1836, just at dawn, the Parker family loaded their wagon and set out on the Old La Bahia Road, northeastward from Fanthorp Inn. Following along behind were the livestock recovered from around Fort Parker, herded by Lorenzo and Luther.

Around mid-morning the group passed through the small community of Roan's Prairie, then turned eastward on a wagon road leading to Huntsville.

The scenic countryside was a grassland prairie of small rolling hills and valleys, occasionally giving way to small creeks lined with dense timbers of oak, elm and other hardwoods.

The procession made good time and by mid-evening of the second day they began to see the immense pine timber forest of east Texas where majestic pines grew to heights of over 130 feet.

Passing through the community of Huntsville, they traveled six miles to the homestead of Jessy Parker. Though not related, they were welcomed as family. Here James was able to obtain a plot of land on the east side of Harmon's Creek and build a home for his family.

*This area of Montgomery County was later renamed Walker County

* * *

For the next two months James desperately tried seeking help from General Sam Houston, Colonel Richard Sparks and Colonel Nathaniel Robbins in obtaining a military company to pursue the Indians and recapture their prisoners, but all efforts were futile.

On a trip to Nacogdoches, after his visit with Colonel Sparks on August 20, 1836, James discovered that his wife's sister, Elizabeth Kellogg, who had been taken captive along with Rachel, had been brought in by some friendly Delaware Indians. They had purchased her from the Ketchaws and were now asking $150.00 for their service. As James was penniless, the money was generously paid by General Houston.

James arrived back at his home in Montgomery County with Elizabeth on September 6th. Patsey, who knew nothing of Elizabeth's return, was overcome with joy in seeing her sister alive.

For the next several days James moped about, pondering what course of action to take in the search for his daughter and grandson. Elizabeth could furnish very little information concerning the other captives or where they had been taken. The prisoners had been dispersed between the various Indian tribes after the raid on Fort Parker.

"James, you're not going to get any help from the Texas government, so I suggest you start checking with the Indian traders up in Indian country to see if they've heard anything about captives," Patsey said impatiently. "With Elizabeth here, and Sarah and Lorenzo nearby, our family will be OK. You need to find Rachel and my grandson."

After spending some time consulting with friends, James was determined to travel alone to Coffee's Trading Post located along the Red River at the mouth of Walnut Bayou in Indian Territory, Oklahoma, a journey of almost five-hundred miles.

Due to Holland Coffee's notable trading abilities among the many nations and tribes of Indians, it was thought he may not only have information concerning captives, but be instrumental in negotiating and arranging for prisoners to be brought in for purchase. Indians were always highly agreeable to trading their stolen livestock and captives for tobacco, knives, guns and whiskey.

James left his home near Huntsville, Texas around the middle of September 1836. Two weeks later he arrived at Jonesborough on the Red River. During his trip through this vast, unsettled part of Texas he was in constant danger of encountering hostile Indians.

At Jonesborough James obtained a fresh horse as his was worn out.

From Jonesborough James proceeded one hundred miles upstream to Coffee's establishment, following a road along the bank of the Red River.

On the evening of the third day he arrived at the post, which was a stockade made of tall log pickets similar to a fort. Riding through the gates he dismounted in front of the trading store and shuffled wearily inside.

The trading house was like any other store with a counter across the back and boxes and barrels arranged along the walls. Items such as colored calico material, beads, earrings, tobacco, pipes, rope, axes and other goods were displayed around and on the counter.

"Well fella, looks like you've come a long way," a gravelly voice declared. "Don't believe I know you. I'm Abel Warren, operator of this station for Mr. Coffee. What can I do for you?"

"I'm James Parker. Come here to see if you might have information on any Indian captives. I'm looking for a seventeen-year-old girl with red hair, she may have a baby boy with her."

"Yeah, we hear about captives. Even manage to ransom a few. But, I can't say I've heard of one with red hair lately. You must be one of the Parkers down in central Texas. Heard about your trouble with the Comanche back in April – May?"

"May 19th," James stated.

"Tell you what you can do. Stick around here a few days. There's Indian traders in and out of here all the time buying supplies to trade at camps up river. You might find out something from them. If you need a place to stay and a meal, see Fitzgerald. He and his wife have a cabin at the far end of the stockade."

On or about the second week in October James received word from an Indian trader of a captive woman bearing the description of Rachel, who had been brought in to Captain Pace's station on the Blue River, some eighty miles distance. With this news James immediately made plans to go but soon found his horse was unable to cross the river. Determined to go on foot he left his horse with Fitzgerald and floated across on a log raft. Finding no road or trail to follow he used his compass to direct his way through the swamps and thickets of the river bottom. During this time he lost most of the bread and meat furnished by Mrs. Fitzgerald. That first night, exhausted, he tried to sleep, but could not due to the thought of being so close to his daughter.

As another night fell over the unbroken prairie James was gathering brush for a fire when a thunderstorm erupted. In moments, sheets of blowing rain fell in torrents. When lightening flashed the prairie appeared to be one solid sheet of water. Having no protection he stood with his back to the pounding rain and his two pistols tucked under his arms in an attempt to keep them dry. Sometime before dawn the wind changed to the north and within an hour his clothing was frozen. Unable to see his compass in the dark to guide his way, he was compelled to walk in a circle in a foot of water.

As soon as it was light enough to see he pursued his journey with little hope of being alive by nightfall because of the extreme cold. By mid-morning his hands and feet had lost all sense of pain.

It was at this time a body of timber came into view. Making slow progress through the two-foot high grass, matted together by ice, he reached the woods and rested. Finding an old dry log he cut a few dry pieces from his shirt, loaded them in his pistol and discharged it into the dry part of the log, striking a fire. With the fire warming his body he suffered the excruciating pain of thawing out.

Three days had elapsed since James had tasted even a morsel of food. Only his fortitude, courage and the hope of soon seeing his lost daughter gave him the strength to pursue onward.

On the evening of the fifth day, just before sunset, James heard a calf bleat. With renewed energy he pushed on in the direction of the sound. Just at dark he found himself at the Pace's house and stumbled up to the door.

"Wh – Who?" Captain Pace sputtered when he opened the door. "Come in! Fellow you look frozen and half-starved. Go over and warm by the fire. Mrs. Pace will get you a hot cup of coffee. Where you from?"

"Thank you sir. I'm James Parker. I left Coffee's Trading Post five days ago in search of my daughter who was captured by the Comanches seven months ago," James explained. "I was told a young lady of her description was here."

"There was a woman brought in a few days ago. She's now at Samuel Marshall's place."

"Did she have red hair? What was her name?" James asked anxiously.

"Her last name was Yorkins and her hair was dark brown."

"That would not be my daughter. Her name is Rachel Plummer," James sighed. His joyful expectation of being reunited with his daughter had now turned to sorrow.

James remained at Captain Pace's for two nights during which he met with some of Coffee's traders who informed him that Rachel was with a band of Indians who were camped about sixty miles away. However, her child had been killed. With renewed determination James set out afoot for their camp, knowing his fate would be torture and death if caught.

Through bitter weather and in a weakened condition James reached the camp on the fourth day, only to find, to his despair, the Indians had been gone for several days. For the next two days he followed the trail left by the Indians, who numbered in the hundreds, to the Red River where they had crossed. In his feeble condition he was unable to swim across.

Having no timber available in which to construct a raft, James was compelled to turn southeastward, following the river downstream. Feeling faint with hunger and fatigue he resigned to the fate of never seeing his unfortunate daughter again.

Just as the sun was beginning to set James saw timber in the distance along the river. Upon entering the woods he spied a skunk in the brush which he quickly killed with a club and soon had it roasting over a fire.

That night his strength was revived and the next morning he set about making a raft of fallen logs tied together with grapevine. By noon the log structure was completed and James, using a long pole, pushed off into the swift running Red River.

The evening sun hung low on the horizon as James pulled his float to the riverbank near Coffee's Trading Post. He now considered all efforts in regaining his child, at this time, fruitless. With winter coming on he spent a few days with the Fitzgeralds to recuperate then retrieved his horse and headed home. It was now November 1836.

James was in a weak, beaten down condition when he arrived home. For the next few weeks he slept a lot and ate all the time.

* * *

James stepped into the log house and quickly shut the door against the frigid north wind. Outside low-slung gray clouds threatened rain. Winter was breaking up into slush and sleet with the usual freezing setbacks. "Looks like we're in for one of those bitter cold late February northers," he said to his wife.

Ambling over to the fireplace he stoked the glowing coals, kindling a small flame in the smoldering embers, then placed on a stick of wood.

"I think you're right," she sighed glancing up from her work. Patsey was busy mending torn shirts while five-year-old Frances entertained baby Martha. Sarah, her husband Lorenzo, James Wilson and their Aunt Elizabeth were still outside milking cows and tending to the other livestock.

"I wonder what our poor daughter and baby boy are going

through right now," Patsey uttered sadly. "They're both probably half frozen in that dreadful north weather, having no decent winter clothing," she fretted almost in tears. "James we've got to do something."

"I know," he muttered. "As soon as we get some better weather I'm taking a trip to Monroe, Louisiana and collect on the money owed me by some merchants. With this cash I can obtain trading supplies to be used in bargaining with the Indians for their captives. Spring will be coming on by then and they'll be a little more inclined to trade their prisoners."

James left his home near Huntsville at the end of February, 1837. Following the Old San Antonio Road he arrived in Natchitoches, Louisiana on the 7th of March. After resting a few days he continued on eastward to Monroe, arriving there the last of March. Collecting his money he set out again for Oklahoma, Indian country, following the main wagon road westward from Monroe. On reaching Russellville he traveled northward to Washington, Arkansas and continued northwestward to Fort Lawson in Oklahoma near the Red River. By the end of April he was again in Indian country, buying supplies from trading houses along the Red River.

It was at the Smith's Trading House he learned, from a Shawnee Indian, that a white woman had been purchased by a man named Sprawling who was a traveling Indian trader for Marshall's Trading House on the Blue River. When James arrived at Mr. Sprawling's camp he was dismayed to discover the woman was not Rachel.

It had now been one year since Rachel, James Pratt, John, Cynthia Ann and Elizabeth Kellogg were taken captive from Fort Parker. Only Elizabeth, ransomed after four months of captivity, was back safe with her family. All others, still in the clutches of their cruel captors, had not been seen or heard from.

With these thoughts in mind, James was more determined than ever to take bolder actions in finding these children. In desperation he made a foolhardy plan to inconspicuously scout out the Indian camps with the hope of seeing captives and gaining their release by sheer cunning. It never occurred to him that his search was stretching out into a great extraordinary feat of endurance past all limits of reason. In his stubbornness he simply kept on following one hopeful venture after the other.

Armed with a rifle, four pistols and a bowie knife, James along with a man from Sprawling's camp, set out traveling deep into the haunts of Comanche country. Knowing if caught, they would be subjected to hideous torture before being killed.

It was the custom of Indians to make prisoners carry all the water when camped near a stream or river. The two men's brave but risky plan was to conceal themselves near Indian encampments until after dark. When the Indians began dancing, as was their custom every night, they would creep to a point near the water and leave notes, hopefully to be found by the captives, telling of a prearranged meeting place. If caught by the Comanches, the two men would be subjected to hours of unthinkable torture in front of the captives before being killed.

At sundown on the third day of traveling the two men set up camp, hobbled their horses and lay down on the ground to rest. Not long afterwards Indians could be heard trying to steal their horses. James grabbed his rifle and shot an Indian no more than ten feet away. Taking his pistol he shot another. He and his companion scrambled to their horses and fled, riding all night.

As day was breaking the next morning the two men rode into an unexpected Indian ambush. A rifle cracked sending a slug grazing the cheek and ear of James. Quickly shouldering his rifle, James shot one Indian then drew his pistol and shot another. His companion took care of the third one. Not far off they heard yelling 'like the demons of hell'. Without taking time to select a course they urged their horses into a fast gallop and soon left their pursuers far behind.

After this close encounter with the Comanches, James's companion went back to the trading house. This was around the last of May 1837.

James stayed until the first of June, scouting, spying and lurking around the encampments, using his arranged plan, but with no result in communicating with any captives.

During this time he went many days without food, having to move eight to ten miles from the camps in order to shoot game for meat. And always the potential danger of being captured and killed.

Exhausted, ill and hungry James finally decided to go home.

After an absence of five months he arrived back in Montgomery County on June 19, 1837.

Determined to find his daughter and other captives, James made two more trips to the Red River, Indian country, Oklahoma. On one trip, in August with his brother Joseph, they had traveled about five hundred miles when they were forced to return home due to the excessive heat and lack of proper food and water.

On his final tour James found the traders had no information of captives. Ill and exhausted he arrived back at his home on October 28, 1837.

It had now been seventeen months since Rachel was taken prisoner. James had traveled thousands of miles and spent hundreds of dollars and still had made no progress in recovering his daughter. There was not even one clue as to where she was or if she was even alive.

* * *

Luther Plummer, Rachel's husband, also made several tours searching for his wife. He, like James, suffered many hardships and adversities from harsh inclement weather, exhaustion and loneliness in the uncharted, wilderness of Indian country. At one time he was seriously injured from a fall but was fortunate to be found and cared for by a Mexican sheepherder until he regained his health.

While he and James were combing the boundless areas of north Texas and Oklahoma Rachel was hundreds of miles to the north in the rugged Rocky Mountains of New Mexico, Colorado and Wyoming.

PHOTO SECTION

Replica of Old Fort Parker on the original site near Groesbeck, Texas

Christmas festivities at Old Fort Parker, 2010

Replica of Pilgrim Primitive Baptist Church and cemetery, established by Elder John Parker in 1834 near Elkhart, Texas

Christmas festivities at Old Fort Parker

Parker Memorial. Grave site of six victims of 1836 massacre

Plummer Cemetary near Groesbeck, Texas

A Glimmer of Hope
April 1837

Rachel let the pole she was using to dig roots fall to the ground, then plopped down on a large rock, exhausted. The sun was now high in the sky turning the crisp cold morning in the Rocky Mountains to a more pleasant mid-April day. Looking down at her throbbing cracked and calloused hands, still showing deep tender scars around her wrists, Rachel thought, *Oh Lord, how much longer must I remain in this miserable life.*

She had now been with this band of Comanches for a year. Twelve months of enduring inconceivable physical and mental abuse at the hands of her two selfish taskmasters. Suffering from never healing wounds and agonizing grief brought Rachel almost to the breaking point.

With early spring approaching the Indians had turned toward the coolness of the rugged blue mountains with their towering snow covered crowns. Looking upward Rachel could not help being in awe at the grandeur of these majestic mountains with craggy peaks, grassy slopes and piñon dotting hills. A sight surpassing all descriptions.

The brilliant sun had now transferred the brisk morning into a lovely warm day. Stretching far across the mountain's foothills, flowers in a dazzling array of colors were beginning to blossom. Trees growing in the canyons showed signs of leaf buds striving to sprout forth. Everywhere was signs of spring. *What a peaceful place*, she thought.

Gazing toward the mountain ridge her eyes fell on two enormous boulders situated in such a position as to almost conceal an opening in the mountain.

Being both puzzled and curious Rachel trudged up the rocky hillside to the massive stones. Picking her way through the brush around their base she stumbled up to the mouth of a huge cave. Cautiously she inched her way just inside. It was not the fear of the unknown lurking in the darkness which stopped her from advancing farther, but the fear of her mistress's wrath if done so without first seeking her permission.

Dying to explore the cave Rachel scrambled back down to where she had left her root basket. Shouldering the heavy basket she hurried to the village to seek out her mistress.

"Wa'ipu. I have filled my basket and would now ask that you allow me to enter a cave I discovered not far from where I was working," Rachel uttered timidly.

"You worthless white girl," the old mistress screamed. "You are to work, not sleep in a cave. Go bring me water from the river. I am very thirsty."

"Wa'ipu, I will work much harder and gather more roots if you would allow me to go only for a short time," Rachel pleaded.

"You ungrateful servant! I will see to it that you always have much work. You will not have time to enter caves," her mistress snarled in a bitter sharp tongue.

Dejected, Rachel picked up a water pouch and ambled off toward the river. *I'll make my request known to her later. After her mid-day nap she'll be in a better mood,* she reasoned.

Later that evening Wa'ipu relinquished, but only if Taabe was taken along. Rachel did not want to be burdened with her young mistress but had no choice.

Returning to the lodge she immediately made preparations for her adventure. With buffalo tallow she formed several large candles which she placed in a deer skin satchel along with extra tallow, deer jerky and necessary instruments for striking fire.

The next morning, at the first glimmer of dawn, Rachel and her young mistress set out for the cave.

With only the dim light of a candle they proceeded into the dark cavern. After advancing about four hundred feet inside, the walls and ceiling became alive with what appeared to be innumerable stars, from very small to moon sized, twinkling in the blackness surrounding them.

"We are going back!" Taabe ordered desperately in a frightened voice. "This is some type of evil magic! We are getting out of here!" Clutching Rachel's arm she tried pulling her back to the cave's mouth.

"Let go of me! There's nothing to be alarmed about." When Rachel tried to pull away her young mistress struck at her with a stick she had been carrying, but missed. Rachel grabbed the stick and knocked Taabe down.

"If you try to force me to go back before I'm ready, I'll kill you!" Rachel shouted at her young mistress. She then picked up the still flaming candle dropped during the scuffle and proceeded on.

"I am fearful of the dark!" Taabe sobbed. "Please take me back."

Finding it impossible to induce Taabe to follow, Rachel agreed to take her back to the cave entrance, on the condition that she would help her mind the horses at night.

After delivering her mistress back to the cave's mouth Rachel returned to the spot where they had fought, anxious to find the secret of the glittering lights. She soon discovered there were countless crystallized formations embedded in the rock walls and ceiling reflecting the light of the burning candle. With her curiosity now satisfied Rachel began to wind her way deeper into the bowels of the enormous cavern.

Journeying several miles the cave's ceiling and walls began to close in. At one point her progress was obstructed by transparent bar formations, so close together she could not pass between them. Anxious to explore on, Rachel succeeded in breaking one of the bars and entered one of the most spacious and splendid rooms her eyes had ever beheld.

The circular room was about one hundred feet in diameter and ten feet high, with walls, ceiling and floor being almost transparent. Flowing through the room was a beautiful crystal clear stream about two-feet deep. After crossing the stream Rachel followed it for some distance when she began to hear a loud rumbling sound. Proceeding slowly she soon came to where the stream fell off to an immense depth, producing a deafening roar.

Exhausted, Rachel lay down on the ground to rest. She imagined she could hear the dying screams of her baby boy in the deep rumbling roar of the waterfall. Drifting off to sleep Rachel's thoughts returned to home, and the family she would never see again.

As she dreamed, her body appeared to be bleeding afresh from the many wounds inflicted by her cruel captors. In her dream the form of a human being emerged holding out his hand then began bathing her wounds with a soothing liquid, which removed all pain. He then comforted her with kind words, giving strength to the weakness of her body.

When Rachel awoke in the blackness of the cavern she began to pray and give thanks.

He who comforts the afflicted and gives strength to the weak, that God, in His bountiful mercy could have extended His hand to a poor wretch like me, whilst thus buried in the earth. How inscrutable are thy ways, Oh, God; and thy mercy and wisdom, how unsearchable. *

Searching around in the darkness she located her satchel and re-lit her candle for the return trip. Several hours later she stepped out into the bright rays of the evening sun. Finding many footprints at the cave she knew the Indians had been looking for her.

She reached the village just at sundown and was astonished to learn she had spent two days and one night in the cave.

The physical abuse she would receive for being away would be overshadowed by the impressions left on her mind from her stay in the cavern. Those memories were like a healing ointment to her injured soul.

* Rachel Plummer Narrative #21

* * *

"Go back to the village and get our root digging poles," Taabe ordered.

Rachel and her young mistress had set out in the early morning to dig roots and were about a half-mile from their camp when Taabe realized they did not have instruments needed for digging.

Dragging along behind, Rachel was lost in her thoughts. Bone tired and overwhelmed with despair of mind and the endless abuse, she decided the sufferings of this life were not worth living, she began pondering the idea of provoking her captors into killing her.

"Did you hear me? Go back and get our digging poles!" Taabe screamed.

"I'm not going back," Rachel declared.

Enraged Taabe lunged at her with a savage shriek.

Rachel pushed her to the ground and began pounding her in the head with a large buffalo bone found on the ground. The cries of her young mistress pierced the morning air, bringing Indians from the village who gathered around whooping and shouting.

Rachel expected at any moment to feel a spear pierce her heart but was determined to make a cripple of her hateful mistress before they killed her. But, no one touched her. Not one of the Indians attempted to do anything for Taabe or interrupt their fight.

With several cuts about her head freely bleeding, the young mistress began to cry out in a trembling voice for mercy.

Rachel picked up Taabe and helped her back to camp. There she washed and cleaned her mistress's wounds.

Afterward Rachel wondered what dreadful thing the Indians would do now that she had not only disobeyed but hurt her mistress. While she was reflecting on these thoughts an old Chief came by and told her she was a brave fighter and that she must have been directed by the Great Spirit to do good to a fallen enemy when she had the right to kill her.

The old mistress, Wa'ipu, was extremely mad because Rachel had injured her daughter. Stalking up to her, with eyes blazing, she shoved Rachel out of their lodge.

"You are to go get a large bundle of brush and straw!" she stated bitterly.

When Rachel returned with the brush, Taabe told her that Wa'ipu intended on burning her to death. But Rachel had secured a knife and was prepared to take her own life if need be.

The old woman took part of the bundle, set it on fire and threw it on Rachel, blistering her arms and legs. When she went to fling the other flaming bundle Rachel knocked her mistress down and held her in the blaze until she was scorched.

"I will kill you," the old mistress screeched, grabbing a club and hitting Rachel several times. Rachel managed to get the club from her and knocked her down. During their struggle one side of their house collapsed. When Rachel had severely beaten the old mistress she took her into their broken down dwelling and put leaf ointment on their burns.

All during the fight the Indians watched but seemed unconcerned as to what was going on.

The next morning the three women were called to the council house to stand trial before twelve chiefs. Each was allowed to tell her side of the story. When they had finished the elder chief asked the women if they had anything more to say.

"I do," Rachel announced grimly. She then stood up before the twelve chiefs and spoke boldly.

"You did not take me honorably but used a white flag to deceive us. Then you killed members of my family and friends. You have mistreated me, though I have served you faithfully for fear of death. And now, I would rather die than be treated as I have been. The Great Spirit will see that you are punished for your treachery and abuse to me." Rachel then sat down fully expecting the chiefs to order her death.

After conferring with the other chiefs, the elder chief turned to Rachel.

"You are to replace all broken poles of the lodge and Taabe will help you. That is the sentence."

The three women were then dismissed from the council house.

Rachel had learned a valuable lesson here. From that time forward she stood up for herself and fared much better. Still, she was a prisoner and a slave to people who showed no kindness to their captives.

With unquestionable faith in her heavenly Father's infinite love, Rachel prayed He would set her free, even if by death.

The Senoro Plains
May 1837

Leaning back against a tree Taabe picked up a pine cone from the ground and began nibbling on one of its' seeds. *Why is that stupid slave looking up in the tree,* she wondered. Her dark brown eyes were filled with contempt. Taabe's resentfulness toward Rachel stemmed from the lack of control she had over her father's slave. Rachel would often resist her constant demands.

One day, when I am married, my father will give her to me as a wedding gift. I will then show her how a disobedient white slave is to be dealt with, Taabe pouted.

"Get to work!" Taabe shouted. "We cannot be here all day."

Rachel startled from her thoughts, placed the edge of her horn scraper against the tree trunk and commenced peeling off sections of bark, being careful not to girdle the tree.

She had been gazing upward, amazed at the towering height of the tree whose top seemed to reach into the clouds. The Indians called the trees, in this part of the Rocky's, 'Long-Live' trees. Rachel suspected they were the enormous Ponderosa Pine she had heard about.

During the springtime Comanche women harvested the sweet inner bark for food and medicine. The cambium layer, which smelled like vanilla, was cut into sections and rolled for later consumption.

"Wa'ipu said you were to help. Why do you always leave the work to me?" Rachel protested. "You made a promise while we were in the cave to help me with the horses, but you never have."

"You are the slave. Not me. You will be a slave for me the rest of your life. The god you pray to cannot help you. You will never be free. Get to work or my mother will beat you for not having full baskets," Taape stated with a nasty sneer.

Rachel was sure there would be no beating. Her ration of food may be cut or some other punishment, but neither Wa'ipu nor Taabe had attempted to strike her since their big fight. They now resorted to throwing rocks or sticks, which she threw right back.

For the next hour Taabe rested against the tree watching Rachel peel large hunks of bark from one tree before going on to the next.

Working the chunks from tree trunks brought excruciating pain to Rachel's dry and cracked hands, which now had the appearance of belonging to an old woman. Her body, drained from never-ending labor, was haggard and bent having little resemblance to a youthful eighteen-year-old.

As she toiled in removing the bark, its' delightful aroma brought back thoughts of home and the savory smell of fresh-baked wheat bread. How her taste buds longed for the flavorful meals of newly gathered garden vegetables and home-cooked bread.

"Oh my dear Lord, please help me. I cannot linger on thoughts which open anew the fountain of grief to my agonized heart," Rachel murmured softly. "I am in lonely exile, in bonds of slavery, haunted day and night with images of my little children and tortured with thoughts of home. Only You, my God, know why and how it is I am still alive. And, in Your infinite wisdom will decide the time of my deliverance."

At last the baskets were filled to the top and the two girls, captive and captor, make their way down to the Indian campsite along a river flowing out of the Rocky Mountains.

Every few days the squaws along with their slaves, packed their tents and other goods on a travois and moved several miles downriver to a new camp.

Most of the captive slaves of this tribe of Comanches were Mexican women. Rachel was the only white among them. The captive Mexican children were not used as slaves but given to Indian families to raise as their own. The boys were brought up as Comanche warriors. When the girls reached the age of fourteen to sixteen they became the wife of an Indian buck.

Rachel was allowed very little contact with the other slaves but during brief meetings managed to pick up a little Spanish.

After following the flowing river for several weeks the grassy valley began to give way to a dry plain. Here almost every shrub and tree was covered with thorns or briars. What little timber growing was low and scrubby. The Indians and Mexicans called the country 'Senoro'.

It was in this place Rachel discovered a thorn in the shape of a fishhook and strong as one made from metal. With these she caught many fish from the river.

This region of the country was alien to Rachel—strange and mysterious.

On one occasion, while gathering brush from a ravine, she stumbled upon thousands of shining particles lying on the ground. Each of these perfectly transparent rocks was about an inch in circumference and gave off light. On her return to camp with a bundle of brush Rachel noticed that even at a far distance the particles could be seen by the light, which emanated from them. She reasoned they must be diamonds. Later she found out the Indians used them for arrow spikes.

The Comanches had set up their camp near a village inhabited by both Mexicans and Indians. These people cultivated the land and raised corn and potatoes by irrigating from the river.

"I would like permission to go into the village," Rachel said obediently to her old mistress.

"No! You cannot go," Wa'ipu snapped. "Those people do not like Comanches and may do you harm."

It was true the people of the village had no desire to mingle with the Comanches. They were kind people and her old mistress was afraid Rachel would try to find refuge there.

"I am not a Comanche. I am a white slave. I wish only to bargain for corn and potatoes. They will not trouble me."

"Alright, but if you are gone very long your master will send braves to find you and there will be trouble," the old woman warned bitterly. She was eager to have corn and potatoes to eat but was uneasy in going to the village herself.

By hurrying, Rachel made the three-mile journey to the hamlet in less than an hour.

The inhabitants of the settlement only gazed with curiosity at Rachel as she wandered through their colony. Finally she spied an elderly Mexican couple sitting in the shade of their lodge shucking corn and she squatted down near them.

"Good morning," Rachel said in broken Spanish. "I wish to bargain for corn and potatoes."

For several minutes the couple gazed at Rachel with penetrating eyes. "You are a white person, yes? A slave to those Comanches? Where do you come from?" the man asked.

"I am an American. I was taken captive from my home in Texas. I wish to be purchased. My father has much land. He will reward you greatly," Rachel stated, again in broken Spanish and not sure if they understood.

"Too far. Too dangerous," the elderly man said. "White people want only to kill all Mexicans and Indians. They do not like us. You must wait until traders come to your camp. Maybe they will buy you."

Rachel managed to trade animal skins for the basket of corn and potatoes. Leaving the village she had a feeling that all hope of being free from the brutality of slavery had vanished.

That evening as Rachel prepared a corn, potato and meat soup her thoughts returned to the village people. Living in a poor desolate and forsaken land, these Indians were some of the healthiest humans she had ever seen. Good people who worked hard cultivating the soil, wanting only to be left alone.

It is no wonder they fear and hate the white Americans who seem determined to drive them from their lands, Rachel reasoned.

During these days, while camped near the Mexican and Indian town, Rachel's opinion of the western native Indians began to change – even to those who held her captive. However this conviction of acceptance was short lived.

A few days later, when the Comanches were moving their camp back toward the Rocky Mountains a group of their braves attacked the village, stole horses and killed those who resisted.

These people are completely strangers to anything like mercy or sympathy, Rachel thought. *They show neither compassion nor emotion unless one of their own is killed in battle. Then they become enraged, especially if the dead are scalped.*

When a Comanche warrior died in battle every effort possible was made to retrieve his body before the enemy could take the scalp – even to the extent of others risking their own lives. Scalps were taken from enemies and kept for good luck.

"Wa'ipu, do your people not know it is wrong to rob and kill people who mean you no harm?" Rachel said to her old mistress.

"Is it right for your people to burn our lodges, killing men, women and children, then take over the land we have lived and hunted on since the beginning of time. Does your God, who you pray to, reward your people for such acts?" Wa'ipu answered in a tight voice.

"No."

"This is our way of life. Do not condemn what you do not understand. Now get back to work."

About a month after leaving the land of thorn covered bushes the band of Indians Rachel was with got in a war with the Osage Indians and several Comanche braves were killed. The Osage cut off the head of some, others they scalped. The Comanches grieved more for the ones scalped.

In this battle the few Osage Indians killed were picked up and brought into the Comanche camp.

"Are they planning to burn or bury those Indians," Rachel asked her old mistress.

"Neither. We will cook and eat them," Wa'ipu declared. "You must help cut them up so the meat can be roasted.

"I – I! My master told me to go check on the horses," Rachel stammered. "I must go now or he will punish me," she lied. Rachel was horrified to think of cutting up a dead human.

"If you are gone long, I will punish you myself," Wa'ipu warned bitterly.

Rachel had no intention of going back soon. *I don't care how much they punish me,* she decided.

Sitting on a rock watching the horses Rachel shuddered at the dreadful thought of cooking and eating a human being.

She had been gone for almost an hour when Taabe came looking for her.

"You better get back to the camp now! My mother is very angry and will probably beat you," Taabe said while munching on a chunk of meat.

Rachel cringed. "Is that a piece of human?" she asked frowning.

"Yes. A foot. The hands and feet are the most delicious parts. Here. Try some." she said with a smirk, offering the foot to Rachel.

"I am not hungry," Rachel declared dryly, and started back toward the encampment. *That is hideous,* she thought in disgust. *How could they be so vile as to be fond of eating another human. Only inhuman cannibals would eat the flesh of another person with no more concern than if it were a piece of buffalo meat.*

That night, while Rachel watched over her masters' horses and brooded over the wickedness of the human race, her thoughts returned again to her little boy who had been snatched from her bosom at the young age of eighteen-months, never to be seen again. The scorching recollection of his anguished cry for his mother started a flood of painful emotions. He now would be almost three years old. *Where had they taken him? What had they done to him? Would he grow up to be one of them – a cruel savage? Would he remember his mother?* These thoughts tore at Rachel's heart.

With tears streaming down her face Rachel dropped to her knees. Looking up into the star lit heavens she pleaded with her maker.

"Precious Lord, I beg of you to consider my little James Pratt. Place him into Your protective holy hands. I appeal to Your tender mercies that he be returned to our people. If not, please guide his dear life into a manhood of peace and empathy for all humankind. Your will be done in his life and mine."

"My Holy Father I am but a mortal vessel in Your hands. Please help me to remember that my captors are a part of humanity, created by You in Your own image. That as a slave, I am to obey my master. To do good to those who mistreat me. To pray for those who spitefully use me and persecute me. Whatever befalls me, my life is in Your hands. I want to be counted as Your good and faithful servant. Thank You my Lord."

Ransomed
June 1837

Rachel set straight up with a jolt. Blissful happiness flooded her very soul as though she had been raptured into the heavens.

Was it a dream or a vision? An angel in human form, like the angelic being in the cave, appeared to her. With four outstretched wings he lifted her up and delivered her into the waiting arms of her father and mother.

Rachel threw off the buffalo cover and stood up in the cool, pre-dawn darkness. Gazing upward to a host of twinkling stars she slowly sank to her knees. Raising her hands toward the brilliant artistic heaven she gave praise to her Savior.

"Thank you my Father for showing your servant a vision of my deliverance, which has renewed my faith of your eternal compassion for your children. I now know, with full confidence, that in your infinite wisdom have established beforehand my redemption, and whether now or in the future will once again be returned to my family." What joy Rachel felt kneeling in the silent gray light of morning giving praise to her Lord and Master.

It was now the middle of summer but the frosty mountain air sent chills through Rachel's weak frame. With a renewed spirit she picked herself up from the ground. Wrapped in the buffalo cover she set out to check the horses.

For the rest of the day Rachel labored cheerfully at her never ending chores with rekindled energy, even finding some pleasure, not drudgery, in her many tasks.

That evening as she toiled at scraping buffalo hides Rachel noticed Mexican traders coming in to the Comanche's camp and setting up tents for trading their merchandise. With hopeful anticipation she watched as one of the men walked in her direction.

He was a stocky, barrel chested man dressed in tattered dusty trousers, boots and a buckskin coat. His dark greasy hair spilled out from under a wide brimmed soiled hat. With an expressionless face, half hidden by a drooping mustache, he looked fearsome.

"Do you wish to be purchased?" he asked abruptly in broken English.

Rachel, so astonished at hearing English being spoken, sat speechless staring at the Mexican trader with her mouth gaped open. She understood what he said but no words would leave her mouth.

"I said. Do you wish to be purchased?" the trader said in Spanish.

Again Rachel understood but being so taken by surprise was unable to utter a word.

Baffled, the trader spoke in Comanche. "If you wish to be purchased take me to your master."

"Yes! Yes!" Rachel declared desperately, bolting to her feet. "Come! Come with me! I will show you!"

They soon found the old Indian and the trader asked if he would sell his captive. No word that ever reached Rachel's anxious ears sounded so dear as the treasured reply of 'Yes' from her master. Her sick and run-down body trembled with anxious joy.

The trader made an offer, which the old Indian refused. He then sweetened the offer more but her master still refused.

"I can give you no more!" the Mexican trader announced impatiently. When Rachel heard those words her broken heart throbbed within her breast and tears began to well up in her eyes.

"Please, my Holy Lord, intercede for me," Rachel begged silently.

"I will make you one more offer," the trader said at length.

At this offer her master agreed and one of the other traders was sent back to their tents to gather the merchandise. As he delivered the articles to the old Indian, Rachel's frail and emaciated frame overflowed with joy.

A thousand thoughts filled her mind as she walked to her new master's tent. With thanksgiving she cried out, in her heart, to her God who always hears the pleas of his children.

My God was with me in distress, My God was always there; Oh! May I to my God address thankful and devoted prayer. *

She was soon informed by her new master that he would be taking her to Santa Fe, New Mexico.

Sleep came very little that night. But, as Rachel waited eagerly for the first light of day her thoughts were filled with gratefulness to the Devine Guardian of the heaven and earth.

*Rachel Plummer Narrative #21

* * *

Hearing sounds of activity around her tent Rachel got up from her pallet and hurried outside where the traders were packing their horses and mules under the pale blue light of a quarter moon. It would soon be daylight and she would be leaving this place of sorrow and grief.

At first Rachel did not notice her. But, as the dim moon settled on the horizon and the first glimmer of morning filtered through the trees, there was Taabe sitting on a large rock, head down and shoulders slumped. Rachel ambled over, climbed up on the rock and sat down beside her.

For several long minutes they both watched the men ready their horses, saying nothing. As day began to break Taabe jumped down from the rock.

"You have been a good slave. I will miss you," she mumbled looking up at Rachel with sad eyes. She then turned to walk away.

Rachel wanted to tell Taabe that she forgave her and her family for the misery brought upon her, but did not know a Comanche word for 'forgive'. She simply said, "May the Lord of heaven watch over you and your family, keeping you safe and bring peace to your heart."

Taabe glanced back then continued on.

"Woman, are you going to be able to make this trip? You look quite thin and sickly to me. I can see these Comanches treated you pretty brutal," the man who had bargained for Rachel remarked in

Spanish. He was striding toward her leading a saddle horse.

"Yes. Yes. I am fine."

"If you think you can stay on this horse, we are ready to go."

Rachel quickly hopped from the rock and vaulted up into the saddle.

"You are stronger than I thought," he declared showing a toothy grin. "Santa Fe is a long distance. May be a three-week trip. We'll be traveling thirty to forty miles a day. You stay in the saddle and hang on."

As the morning sun peeked up on the eastern horizon a caravan consisting of six men, one ransomed female, pack mules, and a herd of horses bartered from the Indians, made their way southward along a trail in the eastern foothills of the Rocky Mountains. A trip that would last seventeen days.

On the tenth day of their journey Rachel recognized a river they were crossing.

"What is this river called?" Rachel asked. "I have been here before."

"It is the South Platte River," the lead Mexican trader answered. "We will be staying here for the night." At night the Mexicans took turns watching the horses and mules fearing the Comanches would try to steal them back.

In the late evening of the next day the travelers descended a mountain pass into a large valley which stretched southeastward. A rushing river flowed through the valley. Rachel immediately recognized the region.

This is the very place where hundreds of Indian tribes assembled for a war council over four months ago. I was here! Rachel remembered. *This is the Arkansas River.*

"I was here when thousands of Indians met to determine when they would invade and take possession of Texas," Rachel said to the head trader.

"Yes. I heard of their war council. They will do nothing. They only talk. Indians always meet here at the Arkansas to plan war."

Around noon of the twelfth day the party was at the summit of, what the Mexicans called, 'Sangre de Cristo Pass (Poncha Pass)'. It was while moving down the south side that Rachel began to teeter in her saddle. Exhausted and weak her frail body careened forward and slid from the saddle, crumbling to the ground.

Instantly two men sprang from their horses and carried Rachel's listless frame to a small mountain creek and bathed her face in the cool water. The other traders rounded up the horses and pack mules, holding them in a small meadow to graze.

Wearily Rachel set up and looked around.

"I'm sorry," she said in a weak voice. "I guess I was just tired."

"Here, drink," the leader of the group urged, handing her a gourd of water. "We will wait here until you are better. In a few hours we will be down in the San Luis Valley. There you can rest and soak in hot mineral springs. It will help heal your body. You will feel much better tomorrow. My men will kill a buffalo calf for us to eat. It will give you strength."

An hour later Rachel was back on her horse and the travelers continued on, following the creek down into the plains which stretched far across empty space to distant mountains almost hidden in a smoke-like haze.

After an hour of soaking in the hot mineral springs, a tasty meal of tender buffalo meat and a restful night's sleep Rachel felt much better.

The man was right, she thought. *I haven't felt this good in months.*

The group was now making good time. They did not take the route as Rachel's captors had, almost a year ago, but followed a small stream flowing through the great prairie.

Rachel recognized the valley. She still remembered the grassy plains, springs and wildlife abounding. She once saw a herd of buffalo here that was uncountable.

Around mid-morning Rachel began to make out the form of a solid white mountain rising up in the shadow of the east mountain range. When the traders stopped to water their horses and mules she asked about the mountain.

One of the Mexicans reached down and picked up a handful of dirt and let it sift through his fingers. "*Arena*," he said pointing toward the mountain.

"Sand?" Rachel questioned in disbelief. "That's a mountain of just sand?"

Rachel looked at the other men. "Is it true? Just sand?"

The men all nodded, yes.

"How did it get there?" she asked, looking back at the man who told her it was sand.

With a puzzled expression he drew his shoulders upward in a gesture of 'I don't know'.

God does some mysterious things, Rachel marveled.

"When will we reach the Rio Grande River that flows through this valley?" she asked.

"Tomorrow we will cross it."

"Those friendly people living along the river, are they Mexican or Indian?"

"Both. Sometimes the Apache Indians are not so friendly," he warned.

Around noon the next day Rachel began to see a line of trees in the distance. *This has to be the Rio Grande,* she reasoned.

Soon fields, watered by irrigation ditches, came into view. When they reached the river some of the men bartered for supplies while others rounded up the mules and horses to graze near the water.

Here the Rio Grande, which had been flowing eastward, turned to the south. The Comanches, along with Rachel and other captives had once camped along this river farther west.

After crossing, the traders continued on their journey, following the 'Old Spanish Trail' southward. Two days later they were back on the banks of the Rio Grande still flowing to the south. Here they crossed to the east side and set up camp.

"How far to Santa Fe?" Rachel asked the Mexican leader.

"One day. Tomorrow night I will deliver you to the home of Colonel William Donoho. He is the one who paid me to bring you to Santa Fe. He instructed me to ransom you at any cost," the Mexican said with a broad smile, showing white teeth under his dark droopy mustache.

Finally, late in the evening of the seventeenth day the weary travelers were in view of Santa Fe, the capital of New Mexico.

Following a well-used wagon road past sun baked fields and scattered adobe homes, the party arrived at the outskirts of the main town. Here Rachel and her rescuer separated from the rest of the men, horses and pack mules and continued on to the heart of the city following a winding narrow street lined with crowded houses.

The Donoho's massive Spanish style home sat at the far end of the plaza.

"Is this Mr. Donoho's home?" Rachel asked, astonished by its grandeur.

"It is their home and also an inn. Captain Donoho owns this hotel and a trading post. It is the best in all of New Mexico."

To Rachel it appeared to be a majestic mansion for royalty.

When they brought their horses to a halt at the entrance of the stone fence encircling the villa, Rachel's heart skipped a beat and she began to panic.

Who were these people. she wondered. She had neither seen nor spoken to clean, decent dressed, English speaking people in over a year. *What would they think when they saw her – filthy, foul smelling and dressed as a savage.*

All these thoughts flooded Rachel's mind as they walked through a beautiful courtyard of flowery gardens and orchards, in the center of this elegant manor, and up to a large impressive door.

After knocking, a few minutes passed before a well-dressed man opened the door.

"Are – Are you Rachel Plummer!" he stammered, looking both surprised and excited. "Come in! Come in!"

Stepping through the doorway Rachel was immediately taken into the arms of an attractive, elegant lady who embraced her with the warmth of a loving mother for her lost daughter.

"Oh Rachel! You poor child. We are so thrilled you're at last free from the clutches of those horrible people," she uttered softly. "My name is Mary and this is my husband Colonel William Donoho. Welcome to our home. I assure you we will do everything we can to facilitate your return to your relatives," she said cheerfully, leading Rachel into the sitting room, leaving her husband to carry out business with Rachel's rescuer.

That night, for the first time in almost fifteen months Rachel slept peacefully in a soft bed, safe behind the four walls of loving people.

Santa Fe, New Mexico
July 1837

Rachel was awakened by what she thought was the snort of horses. *I've got to get up and tend to the horses.* Opening her eyes, she sat up in bed and looked around. *There are no horses! I'm not with the Comanches! I'm free!*

Streams of sunlight had now begun to peek through the open windows and a cool breeze filled the room with a flowery fragrance.

Rachel stood up beside her bed. Taking off the borrowed nightgown she slipped on the clean Mexican style cotton dress left for her.

With Christian compassion Mrs. Donoho had anxiously sought to comfort Rachel in body and soul.

When dressed, Rachel eased through the door and out into the courtyard's flourishing gardens. Seeing a bench under the orchard trees, she ambled over and sat down, letting the reality of this blissful moment surge through her.

"Good morning," a soft, cheerful voice said. "I see that you're up. Come, I have fresh baked bread and there is someone I would like you to meet." Mrs. Donoho had seen Rachel in the garden and was beckoning her to come.

"Rachel, this is Mrs. Harris," Mrs. Donoho said, as they entered the dining area where the sweet aroma of newly baked bread still lingered.

When Mrs. Harris pushed away from the table and rose to be introduced, Rachel could not help but notice the telltale signs of abuse

101

on her face and arms – disfiguring scars and cuts that had not healed, dark circles around deep-set eyes and crudely cropped hair. It was clear to Rachel, she had been a captive slave among heartless Indians.

"Mrs. Harris was brought to us by my husband's Mexican traders a few weeks ago," Mrs. Donoho continued. "She has been working for an American gentleman, Mr. Smith, doing domestic choirs and making him fine linen shirts. She is working to soon earn enough money to pay her passage on the next large wagon train traveling to Independence, Missouri. "I'll leave you two to get acquainted. I must tend to my three young children."

After Mrs. Donoho left the room the two women sat in silence, tears streaming down their faces, each with knowledge of what the other had been through. Nibbling at a slice of hot bread they occasionally glanced up, neither knowing what to say.

"Where are you from?" Mrs. Harris finally asked.

"Texas," Rachel replied. "My home was at Fort Parker in central Texas."

"I lived in Texas for over a year. It was near the Rio Grande River in south Texas," Mrs. Harris said sadly.

For some time the two ladies sat drinking hot coffee and munching on warm bread. Their conversation was mostly about where they grew up, their family and their friends.

Later they strolled out into the courtyard and sat in the shade. The pleasant chirping sounds of birds fluttering about in the trees had a comforting effect on the two despondent women.

"Would – would you like to tell me how you were taken captive?" Mrs. Harris asked reluctantly.

For several minutes Rachel stared down at the ground. "Yes, I think I would," she uttered sorrowfully, raising her head. "But, I will not tell you of my baby boy's death. I cannot bear the thought."

"They killed my infant baby too. It was a horrible death," Mrs. Harris muttered.

With tears stinging her eyes, Rachel looked over at her new friend and they both began to sob.

When they were able to stop weeping Rachel began telling Mrs. Harris of the raid on Fort Parker, the capture of her and others, the loss of her eighteen month old boy, where she was taken and her long awaited ransom from the Comanches. When she finished Rachel looked at her friend and smiled. It felt as if a small part of the burden she had carried for so long had been lifted.

"I think it is helpful to tell someone who has suffered the same fate and can understand," Mrs. Harris sighed. "Let's walk to the plaza and when we get back I will tell you of my enslavement by the Comanches."

The hot, dry, hard-packed streets of the bustling plaza were in opposite contrast to the beautiful, well-kept, flourishing gardens inside the walls of the Donoho's stately dwelling.

One story adobe shops, where Mexican vendors gathered to sell fruits, vegetables and other goods under long porches, lined the east and west sides of the plaza. On the north side sat the one-story, flat roof Governor's Palace. Behind it stood the walls of the military fort. An adobe church, with elaborate carvings around the roof's edge and bell tower, sat on the south side.

This centuries old town, with its' shabby, crumbling buildings, was the Capital City of New Mexico.

Strolling down the street Rachel would often catch a glimpse, through alleyways, of spacious homes with courtyards of trees and flowers.

"Who owns those lovely homes?"

"Americans mostly," Mrs. Harris answered. "They own many shops and other businesses here and around town, also the large farms outside of the city. Most are very caring and generous Christian people. You will soon come to realize their kind supportive compassion for our safe return to our families. The Mexican and Pueblo Indian people who have lived here for hundreds of years, now work for the Americans. They see them as necessary but, to some extent, unwelcome guests."

When the two women returned from their stroll along the time worn streets of the age-old city plaza they insisted on helping Mrs. Donoho in preparation of the noon meal.

After lunch Mrs. Donoho suggested to Rachel that she may wish to lie down in her room for a time.

"Rest always improves a person's recovery from deteriorated health," she declared.

It was mid-afternoon when Rachel awoke. Even with a breeze flowing through the windows of the thick adobe house walls, the dry summer heat was sweltering.

Rachel slipped from her bed and ambled out into the courtyard where she found her friend reading to Mary's three small children, sitting on the ground at her feet.

"Alright children, you may go play now," she said, shooing them away. "Come Rachel. Sit here beside me. It's a little more comfortable here in the shade. We can fan ourselves while visiting," she coaxed, handing Rachel a homemade fan.

"I'm so delighted to now have a friend with whom I can share my horrid experience, someone who can relate and fully understand my sufferings. I'm just not sure where to start."

"Why not start when you left New York for Texas," Rachel suggested.

Mrs. Harris sat for a moment to compose herself. With a set gaze, seemingly at nothing, she began her story as though the scenes were unfolding before her eyes.

"My husband and I were living in New York when we read, in a paper, that a Doctor John Beales was seeking families to settle on a large land grant he had obtained in the Republic of Texas. Each family would receive one-hundred-thirty-seven acres of fertile land and a town lot. The settlement would be located near the Rio Grande River in South Texas. The paper also stated the river was navigable making it possible to sell produce from our harvest. Due to the long growing season, two crops a year could be gleaned. Doctor Beales assured us that security would be provided from Indian attacks. Much too late, we discovered all these statements to be false.

As my husband and I had no children at this time we felt this would be a good opportunity for our future.

In November of 1834 we, along with Dr. Beales and many other families set sail for Texas.

Around the middle of December we reached the port of Capano and were there two weeks purchasing wagons, ox-teams and supplies for our journey to the Rio Grande River. For the next two months our company traveled through a primitive wilderness of unknown hazards. As we drew closer to our destination we were warned by

Mexican village people of the dangers before us and cautioned not to proceed any farther.

In March of 1835 our caravan arrived at the Rio Grande and set up our camp on Las Moras Creek, which flowed into the river. Here we built our cabins and planted crops. For the next year we were met with many misfortunes and disappointments. The land was poor and had to be irrigated, producing only a very meager crop. The summer heat was so intense a person had to stay inside most of the day. And, the Rio Grande River was not navigable.

After receiving word of an Indian attack on a village forty-miles away, our entire settlement decided it best to leave this place of misery.

As we were departing, the group I was with elected to set out for San Antonio. The other group headed in the direction of Matamoros. Mrs. Sarah Ann Horn and I were the only women in our group. Sarah Ann had two little boys, four and five years old. My baby girl was only three months old. Due to my sickness of a broken breast (a cancerous condition),Sarah Ann cared for my baby most of the time.

It was probably around the first of April when we arrived at a large lake near the Nueces River. The next morning we were attacked by a band of Comanches. All the men were killed including my husband and Sarah Ann's husband. Only myself and my baby, and Sarah Ann and her two boys were left alive. We were placed on horses and taken about two miles to their camp of several hundred Indians. Here we were ill-treated by those abusive savages.

We were about to leave this place when one of the Indians decided to kill my baby girl."

Mrs. Harris paused for a moment to compose herself. While she did not elaborate on how the baby was killed, the vision of her baby being snatched from Sarah Ann's arms and it's innocent little body hurled into the air over and over until life was no more, tormented her very soul.

"It was at this point my husband and a German were brought into camp. I thought they had been killed but they were only wounded. The men were stripped entirely naked and bound hands and feet to a post driven into the ground. With their captives in this position, hundreds of shrieking Indians began a demonic dance around their

two bleeding victims."

Mrs. Harris again paused. Her eyes brimmed with tears and her lips began to tremble. Rachel waited for her to continue. For several minutes she tried to speak but could not. The horrifying vision of what had happened was too ghastly for words.

At last she was able to compose herself.

"The Indian warriors forced us to watch while each warrior, in turn, broke from the line and sliced a portion of scalp from the head of my husband and the German. Oh, their pitiful agonizing cries and groans tore at my heart until I was sick. Not wanting to look I hung my head and shut my eyes from the gruesome sight. I was immediately grasped by my hair and compelled to stare directly at my poor withering husband while the sadistic savages pulled strips of skin from his body."

Mrs. Harris covered her ears with her hands and bowed her head, trying to block out the tormenting screams of the two men. Finally she was able to mutter. *"They were shot full of arrows until dead."*

Rachel had never been a witness to such cruelty but knew it was common practice among the Indians to torture men captives in this manner.

For a long period of time the two women sat silently reflecting on unspeakable sufferings of the past year. Wiping away tears, Mrs. Harris raised her head and began to speak softly.

We were then stripped of everything we had, except our dresses and placed on horses. The two little boys, Joseph and John, were stripped naked. Day after day we traveled north westward, following rivers and streams, staying only one to three days in any one place while the warriors raided and killed.

About a month after being taken captive the Indians broke off into three bands of about a hundred each. I was separated from the others. Later I learned the boys were taken from their mother and placed apart in different tribes.

A few weeks ago, around the first of June, Mexican traders ransomed me and brought me here to Santa Fe.

As you can readily envision the harrowing abuse and agony I suffered at the hands of my captors, I will not go into any detail of the vile-treatment I received."

Several minutes passed before Rachel spoke.

"Do you know what happened to Sara Ann Horn and her two little boys?"

"As far as I know they are still with the Comanche Indians," Mrs. Harris replied sadly. "We need to pray for their safety."

With an orchard tree shading them from the hot afternoon sun the two women knelt on the ground in front of the bench.

* * *

The restful days spent in the comfort of the Donoho's home brought renewed strength to Rachel's worn and sick body. But with the passing of each long day she grew increasingly weary, longing for the time she would be reunited with her family.

During this time of waiting, the kind people of Santa Fe donated $150.00 to finance her return to Texas, only to have it pilfered by a dishonest priest. The news of the shameless act was a heartbreaking disappointment to Rachel. She must now find some means of earning money for passage on a trader's wagon train, which could take months or even a year.

Distressed but not without hope, Rachel's unshakeable faith gave assurance that her Heavenly Father, who had delivered her from the clutches of the evil ones, would now provide a way for her return to loving family and friends.

The Santa Fe Trail
August 1837

The sun had not yet appeared in the sky as the predawn gray light entering through the open window illuminated the room sufficiently for Rachel to hurriedly dress. *What is going on,* she wondered.

She was awakened by loud sounds coming from outside—the braying of mules, rattling of chains and confused talking of Spanish speaking men.

"Good morning young lady," Mr. Donoho said with a nod as Rachel stepped out into the cool morning air.

Four empty wagons had been pulled up to the courtyard entrance and several Mexican men were unhooking mules, leaving the wagons.

Looking confused Rachel stuttered, "Are – are – we - ?"

"We'll be loading our possessions and leaving for Independence, Missouri tomorrow morning," Mr. Donoho stated firmly. "Mrs. Donoho has breakfast prepared. She'll explain everything to you and Mrs. Harris while you're eating. Your help will be needed in packing."

Independence, Missouri! That's not Texas. But it is the United States, Rachel thought. Excitedly she hurried into the dining area to join Mrs. Donoho and Mrs. Harris.

"Is everyone going? Are you and Colonel Donoho moving to the United States?" Rachel blurted out anxiously in a muffled voice, careful not to wake the children.

"Sit down and have some breakfast and we'll discuss the ongoing events and our plans for leaving Santa Fe," Mary Donoho urged. "Yes, due to the unrest here in Santa Fe, Captain Donoho and I will be moving to Independence, along with many other American families. You and Mrs. Harris may travel with us and seek out your families from there. Both of you will be of much needed help along the way.

I'm sure you both are aware of the turmoil taking place, not only here, but in all of New Mexico. The friction between the Pueblo Indians and the ruling Mexican government has escalated into an outright revolt by the poor Indians against their Hispanic oppressors, whom they hate. As you may know, many of the Pueblo Indians despise the American people living here as well.

This upheaval came to a head last week when the new governor of New Mexico, Colonel Albino Pérez, imposed new taxes. This led to an uprising of the Pueblo Indians. To stamp out this revolt, Colonel Pérez mustered together a small army of around two-hundred men and marched against them, but was ambushed by over a thousand Indians. Colonel Pérez was killed and his body brought back to Santa Fe by the rebel Indians and dragged through the streets."

Mrs. Donoho paused for a few moments to gather her composure.

"Captain Donoho and I have made this place our home for over four years. We have raised our family here and established a successful trading business. But now it's time to leave."

For several minutes the ladies sat in silence. Finally Mrs. Harris spoke.

"Mary, Rachel and I are both ready and anxious to leave this place. Just tell us what to do and it will be taken care of. You and your husband have been our saviors. And now, your gracious generosity extends to offering transportation to the United States, knowing we have very little money to finance our way. How can we ever repay you?"

"Your safe return to relatives will be our reward. Now, there is much to be done," Mary declared. "Captain Donoho is seeing to the loading of wagons at the trading house. It will be our responsibility to gather our belongings, household goods and sufficient food and supplies for a two-month long journey. We will need to see that our Mexican workers pack them securely in the wagons. Rachel, as your health has not fully returned, I would like for you to take charge of my children. When they are dressed and fed, help them in placing their clothing and other possessions neatly in traveling bags." Mary had two daughters, ages five and four, and one three-year old son.

"When that is done you may take the children for a walk or read to them. Also, a noon meal must be prepared."

The last rays of a fading sun were dipping below western mountain tops when the final article was tightly placed aboard an overloaded wagon. Sadly, many pieces of Mary Donoho's beautiful furniture had to be left.

Tomorrow would be the beginning of a two-month, eight-hundred-fifty-mile journey across a treeless plain, inhabited by hostile Indians. Rachel's thoughts were not of the many perils that lay ahead, only of the joyous reunion with her family.

That night, tired and weary from the days exertion she lay awake on a straw pallet contemplating the event that lay ahead.

"My Holy Father in Heaven, hallowed be Your name," Rachel uttered softly. "Lord, I put my trust in You. You alone can deliver me to my father's house. Do not let my faith falter. Never the less, Your will be done in my life."

* * *

The hot August sun was starting to surface over the mountains when the last of forty Conestoga wagons, pulled by a team of six powerful mules, rolled in to join the assembly of heavily loaded wagons in the plaza of Santa Fe. Their destination – Independence, Missouri.

With whips cracking and teamsters shouting, some 240 mules and oxen leaned into their harnesses, setting in motion the long hazardous trek eastward over the Santa Fe Trail.

After three days of bumping and jolting over a rugged and winding mountain road the wagon train moved down out of the Glorieta Pass into the Pecos River Valley. It would be another day before reaching the river crossing at San Miguel.

San Miguel, a small Mexican village on the west bank of the Pecos River, served as the 'port of entry' for collecting taxes on all goods coming into New Mexico over the Santa Fe Trail. The tax on each wagon crossing the river to San Miguel was exorbitant. There was no tax on wagons going east.

The wagon train crossed the river to the east side and set up camp along its bank.

"What are those," Rachel asked Mrs. Donoho, pointing to an area littered with burnt piles of wood and metal. She and Mrs. Harris had been helping unpack goods for preparing an evening meal.

"That's what's left of a wagon train the Indians attacked," one of the drivers standing nearby declared. "Happened last year about this time. Hundreds of savage Comanche warriors swooped down out of the mountains and that's all's left. Never know when those devils will strike." After making these grim remarks he walked away so Rachel and the others could not see the grin pulling at the corners of his mouth.

"Don't listen to him," Mrs. Donoho stated. "Some of these tobacco chewing reprobates have nothing better to do than frighten people. Those are burnt tradesman wagons alright. But, they were probably old and near empty of goods used on the trip from the United States when they arrived here at the crossing. To keep from paying a tax on the wagon, its cargo was switched to other wagons and the empty one set on fire."

Even though it was only a wisecracking joke by a hard-hearted man, fear surged through Rachel as a horrifying picture of the Indian attack on Fort Parker flashed through her mind. She could still hear the bloodcurdling yells of the Comanche warriors, the anguishing cry of her dying uncles and the heart-wrenching scream of her little boy when they jerked him from her arms. She knew the Comanches well, having no doubt that the ugly yarn told by the mule driver could very well befall their wagon train before reaching Missouri.

When Rachel looked into the blurry, tear stung eyes of Mrs. Harris she knew her friend was thinking the same thing. "We're going to be alright," she uttered softly, embracing her friend. "We have seventy to eighty armed men to protect us. I'm sure our Lord will see us safely through."

It was not yet daylight when Rachel crawled out from under her quilt and, in the darkness of a star-lit sky, rekindled the night's fire. Each day was the same. Up before daybreak, cooking a quick meal and being ready to move out at the crack of dawn. Depending on the terrain, the intensity of the August heat and the availability of water and grass for the livestock, the caravan hoped to travel ten to eighteen miles a day.

To help lighten the wagonload, especially in rough and steep country, the passengers often walked, out to the side of the wagon. This also gave opportunity for stretching their legs and staying clear of the blanket of dust billowing out from under the wagon wheels.

"Look at that tall mountain over there," Rachel commented. "It appears to just rise up out of the plains." She was pointing southward to a peak with a relatively small plateau.

The wagons had now come to a stop for a short period of time to rest the team.

"I heard some traders call it Starvation Peak. They said settlers were chased up the mountain and held there on the mesa, surrounded by Indians, until they succumbed to starvation," Mrs. Harris stated.

"That's just a legend," Mary Donoho said, she was standing nearby and overheard their conversation. "You can't believe what those men tell. They'll make up anything to taunt you. I doubt any truth to that tale. You ladies—" Just then the call sounded to 'move out'. " —get aboard the wagon."

It was late evening when the caravan of wagons arrived at the Gallinas River to camp for the night, they were now only a few miles from the village of Las Vegas. From their camp on the river the sheer cliffs of Hermit's Peaks could be seen dominating the western sky.

The next morning, not long after daybreak, the forty wagon procession clambered through the Las Vegas Plaza, the main center of town. On each side of the city square, village people watched the line of wagons rumble by, shouting and cheering them on.

Passing through the town Rachel noticed the square was surrounded by buildings which would serve as fortification in case of an Indian attack.

Having ample provisions for their journey, the train did not stop but pressed on for the small settlement of La Junta, eighteen miles north, at the junction of the Sapello and Moro Rivers. There would be an abundance of water and grass for the livestock and the shade of large cottonwood trees to camp under. It was also the 'jumping-off-point' for wagon trains choosing to take the 'Cimarron Cutoff' of the

Santa Fe Trail, going east to Missouri.

The 'Cimarron Cutoff' was by far the shorter and easier route, but the most deadly. Along with the ever-present danger of an Indian raid, the party of travelers would now be facing an arid, dry and barren land offering little water, grass or firewood for hundreds of miles.

Before leaving the small village of La Junta the next morning all water barrels were filled to capacity. It would take three days of hard traveling over a desolate and dry plain before the travelers reached the rock crossing of the Canadian River. Due to the extreme dry weather there was only a slim chance of finding water at the foothills of 'Wagon Mound', located half way to the Canadian.

It was mid-afternoon of the next day when Mary Donoho pointed out the clear outline ridge of the towering 'Wagon Mound', a mountain seemingly rising out of the desert.

"It does have the shape of a Conestoga wagon!" Rachel said, surprised at what she had been told of this majestic mountain. Wagon trains, coming from Independence, used it as a guiding landmark.

"Maybe water can be found there," Mary said hopefully.

Late that evening the caravan of wagons came to a halt at an arroyo in the shadow of the mountain. But found only a trickling of water. Here they camped for the night. The travelers were now about one-hundred miles from Santa Fe – seven-hundred-fifty miles from Missouri.

Leaving 'Wagon Mound' the wagons turned a more easterly direction. If all went well they would set up camp that night on the east bank of the Canadian River.

As the weeks dragged by each grueling day seemed the same. Up each morning before the crack of day, a quick meal and on the trail at the first light. For long monotonous hours the wagons bumped and jolted across wide treeless plains, literally baked by the scorching sun, which stretched from horizon to horizon. Flat top mountains and peaks of gigantic crags of rugged rock, beaten by wind and weather into weird shapes, rose up out of the otherwise featureless desert. At night camp was made, hopefully near a river or stream. Meals were prepared, guards posted, and the weary, exhausted travelers rested until the starting of a new day.

Hour after hour Rachel sat hunched on a wagon bench. Suffering from prior maltreatment, fatigue and grief she grew weaker, mentally and physically with the passing of each day. Wishing only to daydream of a joyous reunion with family and friends, her thoughts continually reflected back to her children – the hideous death of her infant baby – the abduction of little James Pratt from her grasp, never to be seen again. *Where was he? Was he being treated well? Had he been killed? Why did I not stay with the Indians and continue my search? Why did I not remain in Santa Fe until he could be ransomed? I should not have given up. I abandoned my baby boy!* These things Rachel pondered in anguish over and over. Sorrow and remorse filled her days.

Mrs. Harris, sitting next to her on the bench, knew clearly Rachel's sufferings and empathized with her. She too constantly brooded over the death of her husband and child. The picture of her husband's inhuman torture – stripping pieces of skin from his body before shooting him full of arrows – could not be erased. The heart-wrenching screams of her infant baby as the callous savage flung her helpless body into the air, letting it crash to the rocky ground until she was dead, was permanently etched in her mind.

"Rachel, when the wagons stop to rest the teams, would you like to get out and walk for a spell?" Mrs. Harris asked. "It may help take our minds off the past."

"Maybe, for a short time," Rachel replied, almost reluctantly.

Later the two friends plodded along, with other acquaintances and friends, outside the dust of the forty rumbling and squeaking wagons. Rachel's spirits began to rise as they talked of happier times with loved ones.

The landscape had now changed from the arid desert to dry grassland with gentle rolling hills and small valleys, occasionally finding a few trees in the shallow canyons. With a gentle breeze blowing, the otherwise sultry day seemed rather pleasant.

"Captain Donoho said we would probably make the Arkansas River today, and from there water will be available for us almost every evening when we camp," Mrs. Harris commented.

"I hope he's right," Rachel sighed, thoughtfully. "We haven't seen fresh water since leaving the cool streams of the Cimarron four days ago."

After crossing the Arkansas the caravan continued northeastward over the rolling prairie, finding small streams and grass along the way.

On the fourth day after crossing the Arkansas, they arrived at the junction of the Arkansas River and the Pawnee River. Here large timbers of elm, ash, elder, willow and cottonwood grew, and grass in abundance. Countless buffalo tracks could be seen along the river and out onto the prairie.

One of Captain Donoho's teamsters told him this was Pawnee country, but would only see them if they came to trade. Also, a large buffalo herd had been located and marksmen were sent out. If fortunate to get within range, there would be ample meat for everyone.

"How many days do you think we are from Independence?" Mr. Donoho asked the teamster.

"I'd say twenty to twenty-three, depending on how our wagons hold up. So far we've been lucky," he answered.

Mrs. Donoho and Mrs. Harris, standing nearby overheard the conversation and gave a disappointed look and gesture to each other. The Donoho's three children, who were listening, gave no hint of dismay at the news but were overjoyed at the prospect of seeing buffalo and possibly obtaining a horn, tail or ear.

Day after day, from dawn till dusk, the long chain of wagons rumbled slowly across the grassland plains, with the passing of each day seemingly longer than the day before.

Needing a relief from the incessant wagon vibration, Rachel stood and was about to ask the teamster to stop when she caught a glimpse of what appeared to be a line of trees on the horizon. When the wagon reached a rise in the prairie she could then clearly see a body of trees outlined across the endless savanna of tall dead grass.

"Is there a river up ahead?" she asked the driver.

"Yeah. The Neosho River. The place is called 'Council Grove'. It's Osage-Kaw Indian country. The United States government negotiated with the Indians to allow wagon trains to pass through their land. We'll be stopping for the night. May do some trading. A few folks are low on provisions and it's still twelve to thirteen days to Missouri."

The travelers could not have imagined the beauty of this place called 'Council Grove'. From the burning open prairie they entered under cool shades of century old oaks, elms, maple and hickory, their limbs covered with enormous hanging grapevines, loaded with purple fruit. The strip of Council Grove forest and meadows covered an area one-mile long and one-half mile wide on the east branch of the river.

That evening, many of the travelers eagerly bartered items from their wagon for fresh meat and vegetables from the Indians.

On October 13, 1837, exactly two months after departing Santa Fe, the buildings of Independence could be seen far on the distant horizon, ending their risky, arduous trek across the hostile desert of New Mexico and plains of Kansas.

News of the approaching wagon train reached the city, bringing hundreds of people to line the street, welcoming the weary travelers.

Tears of joy streaked the face of Rachel and Mrs. Harris as the wagons rattled their way along the main road, bordered by hotels, saloons, churches and other businesses, past the courthouse and moving on to the river where an abundance of grass and timber could be found. This would be their final camp while purchasing provisions before going their separate ways.

It was a time of rejoicing for those who were now at their journeys end and safe from their adversaries. But for Rachel there seemed to be no end. Though free from the bondage of Comanche slavery and in the comfort and safety of friends, she was no closer to her home in Texas than when she was in the mountains of New Mexico.

How will I get there? Rachel worried. *How can I travel eight-hundred miles alone, through largely unsettled, treacherous country? Will my weak and exhausted body endure such a trip? My husband, my father, my mother – is there anyone still alive? Will I die before seeing my loved ones? Who will help me now?*

Rachel's strong faith was beginning to falter.

A Joyful Reunion
December 1837 - February 1838

"Rachel! I'll be leaving soon!" Mrs. Harris said eagerly, entering the room she and Rachel shared. "I received a letter from some of my kindred living in Boonville, Missouri. They will be here in a week to take me home with them."

"That's wonderful. I thought you said you had relatives in Texas?" Rachel remarked dryly, turning from the window where she had been watching small squirrels scampering in tall oak trees near the river. Occasionally the top of a steamboat's smokestack could be seen as it passed downstream, her thoughts being not on squirrels or steamboats, but on her Texas home. It had been over two weeks since arriving in Independence and still she was no closer to family than she was in Santa Fe.

"I do have folks in Texas but I hope never to go back there," her friend stated firmly. "I doubt I could live through a trip to Texas. I seem to be a little weaker every day." For the past two months the inflammation of Mrs. Harris's broken breast (cancer of the breast) had slowly spread causing much pain throughout her body.

Saying no more Rachel turned back to again staring out the window. Mrs. Harris placed a doting arm around her companion and they both stood quietly, gazing out the window, seemingly at nothing, while their kindred spirits sought comfort from each other.

During their time here with the Donohos they had received much support and encouragement from townspeople, who also assisted them with donations, for which they were extremely grateful. But still their longing for family could not be quenched.

"I know how hard it is for you at this time. Please strive to hold onto your faith," Mrs. Harris whispered to Rachel. "Just remain faithful and He will see you through. I'll not be here much longer but will not cease praying for your safe return to your loved ones. Be brave my friend. With the Lord's help, I'm sure you will endure through these difficult times."

A slight smile played at the corners of Rachel's mouth when she looked, with tear-filled eyes, at her dearest friend.

"I will miss you."

After Mrs. Harris left to go home with her kin Rachel's anxiety to learn something of her relatives grew so great that at times she was tempted to set out afoot for Texas. All her prayers to Almighty God to intercede and devise some means for her return home seemed to go unheard. Despite the attempts of Mary Donoho to console and council her she could not be comforted. Every moment of not knowing seemed unbearable.

Month after month crept by until it was now December, the dead of winter and very little hope of ever seeing her folks – if they were even alive.

* * *

Huntsville, Texas November 1837

"James, I beg you, please don't make any more trips into Indian country looking for Rachel. We don't know if she's dead or alive," Patsey Parker pleaded with her husband. "You're still ill from past trips. You're killing yourself. I want Rachel back as much as you, but look at what you're doing to the rest of the family. We have no money and very little food. If it hadn't been for neighbors we would've starved to death."

James had returned a month earlier from a long journey, again to Oklahoma Indian country, checking with traders for any information on captives. He was thinking of making another trip.

"What day is this?" James asked from his bed. He still had not fully recovered from all the tours made in search of Rachel over the past year and a half.

"Thirtieth of November, eighteen-thirty-seven," his wife answered. "Rachel has been gone seventeen months. If she and her baby are alive the child would be a year old by now. James Pratt would be near three. Lord I hate to even think of what those savages have done to those poor little children," she grieved.

That night, a little before midnight, there was a loud banging on the Parker's cabin door.

"Who is it?" James called.

"G. S. Parks! I've got word of your daughter, Rachel!"

On hearing this James and Patsey sprang out of bed. While James stumbled to the door, Patsey, with trembling fingers, lit a lamp.

"Come in Parks," James said, opening the door. "What kind of information do you have?"

"Well, sir. I received word from a fellow merchant by the name of Captain William Donoho. His Mexican trader ransomed a lady with red hair by the name of Rachel Parker Plummer from the Comanches. They brought her to his home in Santa Fe, New Mexico. She is now staying with his family in Independence, Missouri. They've been there since the middle of October. Your daughter is eagerly waiting to hear from her relatives."

So overjoyed in hearing her child was alive, Patsey fell into her husband's arms, weeping out of control. By now all of the children were up, gathered around their parents, anxiously asking if their sister was truly alive.

"Is little James Pratt with her?" Patsey questioned when she was finally able to calm herself. "Is there a baby?"

"There was no mention of anyone else being ransomed except a Mrs. Harris who went to live with relatives in Missouri," Parks said awkwardly.

"James, on my way here yesterday I met up with your son-in-law, Lorenzo Nixon. He said to tell you he was leaving for Independence to get Rachel. He didn't think you were in any condition to make that trip. I guess I better go while there's still a full moon. I'm staying with friends a few miles from here. Is there anything I can do for you folks?"

"You've done enough. Thank you for traveling so far to bring us this wonderful news," James declared, eagerly shaking Parks' hand.

"I should be the one going to Independence," James contended after G. S. Parks had left. "She's our daughter."

"James, you know good and well you're not in any kind of shape to travel anywhere and Independence is over nine-hundred miles from here. Just let Lorenzo handle this."

* * *

Independence, Missouri December 1837

It was late afternoon and Rachel had been in her room all day writing and praying.

The gloomy December morning began with icy overcast skies and flurries of snow that dusted the earth with a white powder. Not a day to rejoice in, but a day she could delight in prayer, exalting the Lord for providing His servant a safe and warm haven among friends.

Though she had been waiting for over two long months Rachel knew her Heavenly Father would never forsake her. One day, at His good pleasure, she would leave this refuge in Independence and be reunited with family.

Rachel finished praying, picked up her pen and continued jotting down her thoughts. She had started compiling a narrative of her life with the Comanches at Santa Fe, but found it difficult to write during their long grueling journey to Missouri. But now, here in the quiet, restful atmosphere of the Donoho's large home, she found the time and energy to continue relating the events of her captivity.

Lost in her thoughts Rachel was not completely conscious of talking taking place in other parts of the house until a soft knock rapped at the door.

"Come in," she said, expecting Mary Donoho or one of the many kind-hearted neighbors who often came to visit.

When the door opened a lean, rawboned, roughly dressed man, wearing a well-worn wool overcoat and heavy leather boots, stepped through the doorway, holding a battered hat in his hand.

For a moment Rachel's eyes showed no recognition. When she realized who it was a lump began to form in her throat so great she could not speak.

With a creased brow Lorenzo gazed at the gaunt, hollow-eyed woman, hardly believing this could be the young red-haired beauty of two years ago.

"Rachel?" he questioned.

Rachel was so overjoyed she scarcely knew what to say. With tears flowing she rushed into her brother-in-laws embrace. "Lorenzo!" she finally uttered. "You're alive! My husband – my father – my mother, are – are they still—?"

"Yes, yes. They're all alive, and your sisters and brother. I've come to take you home."

Several days were spent in preparation for their long journey to Texas. Fresh mounts and pack mules had to be obtained. It was the middle of winter and clothing adequate for withstanding the bitter elements of winter weather needed to be purchased.

It was during this time that Captain Donoho made the decision to accompany them to Texas. Taking two of his men and several pack mules loaded with commodities, he planned to bargain with merchants along the way, returning with goods from the south. This would also give him an opportunity to search out a location for a profitable trading post.

The day of their departure finally arrived. For Rachel it was a time of mixed feelings. Thrilled at the possibility of soon being with her beloved family, but saddened at leaving the companionship of a benevolent woman who for the past four months had generously given of her time and affectionate counseling, for which Rachel would always be grateful. With tears of sadness Rachel mounted her horse and waved goodbye.

Lorenzo had explained to Rachel that her family, which included he and Sarah, her husband Luther and her father, mother and three siblings, now lived near the small town of Huntsville, one hundred miles south of Fort Parker. Depending on the weather, the trip of near one thousand miles could take over a month.

The bright fiery sun was beginning to rise over the horizon as the group of riders and pack mules made their way along the main wagon road, leading them southward across Missouri, Arkansas and then into Texas

The morning had started off damp and frigid but with warmth from the ascending sun would soon give way to a clear crisp day.

This is going to be a good day. Rachel reflected.

Day after day the group made their way southward. Sometimes passing farm houses with acres of plowed fields waiting for spring planting and other times stopping at small villages or towns where a good meal and a warm bed could be had. But, more often these settlements were few and far between, leaving them to camp near a stream or river. On blistering cold nights they huddled around a blazing campfire with hunched shoulders watching the flickering flames while telling stories of their travels.

It was during these times Rachel related many of her experiences while a prisoner of the Comanches, – often being so engrossed in telling the story she slipped into the Comanche language.

At night while hovering under a quilt, trying to stay warm and wishing for the warmth of a buffalo robe, Rachel praised her Lord for His goodness. She now understood the loss of her little boys was not the will or work of God but of people who knew no other way but to embrace and follow after the 'evil-one'. It was at these times of rest, thoughts drifted back to her captors and without knowing why, she implored the Heavenly Father to have mercy on their souls. Strange as it seemed, her hatred for the Comanche people began slowly diminishing, a feeling of compassion taking its place.

Each long day Rachel grew weaker and weaker. The thought of seeing her family again was the only thing keeping her in the saddle.

What if I don't make it? She agonized. *Would not that be best? Would I ever be able to live a normal life? How will I ever face my husband and parents after leaving little James Pratt in the hands of those merciless Indians, thinking only of my own freedom? How will I explain it? I can't bear the thought of not being accepted back into the family. Would it not be best if I left this world now to be with my baby boy?*

These and many more thoughts flooded Rachel's mind day after day on this seemingly endless journey.

Finally, on the bitter cold afternoon of February 19, 1838 the weary travelers trudged into the town of Huntsville. Here William Donoho and his men parted from the other two and made their way to a trading post owned by Ephraim and Pleasant Gram. Lorenzo and Rachel continued on, wishing to arrive at Rachel's father's house, two miles east on Harmon Creek before nightfall.

It was late evening when the worn-out horses and pack mule, with their two riders, lumbered into the settlement of Parkers Mill, which consisted of only a few scattered log houses, out buildings and a saw mill.

Exhausted and hungry Rachel's emaciated frame began to tremble, not from exhaustion or the frigid cold weather, but the anticipation of meeting her family. *Will he recognize me? She fretted.. I'm no longer the healthy, fair-skinned, rosy-cheek girl I used to be. I'm nothing now but an ugly skeleton. My once silky-long hair is now dull, brittle and falling out.* Rachel's fear of seeing her parents had escalated.

"Lorenzo, do you think they will recognize me?" Rachel asked in a weak voice.

"Yeah. You're still the same Rachel, just skinnier."

"I'm afraid Luther won't have me after being with those filthy Indians."

"Rachel, that's nonsense. Everyone will be overjoyed to see you and know you are safe, just as I was. Your husband wants you regardless of where you've been or what has happened to you. You're his wife. He will never leave you," Lorenzo assured. "Look up ahead! That's your home where your family is waiting with open arms."

Rachel lifted her head and looked far down the wagon road where Lorenzo was pointing to a large log house with columns of smoke curling from the chimney.

"See that boy coming from the barn. That's James Wilson, your ten-year-old brother. Look, he sees us!"

The boy dropped what he was carrying and raced for the house crying, "Rachel is here! Rachel is here!"

Luther, who also was coming from the barn, broke into a run to meet them. Before the horses could come to a full stop he lifted his wife's lightweight body from the saddle and carried her toward the house while they embraced.

Oh my beloved husband. How could I have doubted you would not want me, Rachel marveled, snuggling in his strong arms while their tears of joy mingled.

Luther released his wife from his arms so she might stand to be greeted by her family. Rachel's gaunt frail body trembled with intense emotions so great she could hardly stand.

Patsey, deliriously overcome at seeing her daughter, wept uncontrollably.

Rachel's long and perilous journey was over. She was now safe – free from the bondage of slavery from a cruel people. Home at last with caring and loving family and friends. But the grief for her baby boy, whose bloody body, lay buried in the vast regions of the Rocky Mountains, and the loss of little James Pratt, could never be erased. These burdens of the heart, like the scars of her body would be carried to the grave. Would a happy life ever await her? Only her Lord and Master knew. She would trust Him.

How chequered are the ways of Providence. Though my sorrows and sufferings, for the past two years, have been greater than it would be thought human nature could bear, the joy I felt that night overbalanced them all, whilst I poured forth to Almighty God, the humble thanks of a grateful heart for the merciful deliverance of my child from cruel bondage.

How truly does the inspired writer say, that "He that chasteneth when it seemeth fit, and maketh the sorrowful heart rejoice in due season. *

* The James W. Parker narrative #23

Fleeing Adversities
November 1838 – December 1838

Hearing the faint rhythmic drumming of galloping horses approaching, Lorenzo opened the door and stepped out on the porch into the gray light of a cool overcast November morning. The falling temperature being kept at bay by the low-slung layers of sticky clouds.

Moments later six riders, with rifles held across their saddles, appeared around the tree lined bend of the wagon road. From the distance Lorenzo did not recognize anyone but knew who they were. These and other vigilante groups, who called themselves 'regulators' were self-appointed watchmen over a section of central Texas. Acting outside the law, they established themselves as judge, jury and avenger, punishing whomever they determined had committed a crime.

This was the reason Lorenzo and his wife, Sarah, came to stay here with his father-in-laws family while James and Luther were away hauling lumber to the growing town of Montgomery, thirty miles south.

Over the past year growing rumors, accusing James Parker of wrong doings and criminal activities had been spreading. These accusations had increased to the point of linking James with the Indians who murdered Mrs. Taylor and her three children living at Roam's Prairie. It was also alleged he had stolen some horses.

Lorenzo quickly reached inside the door and retrieved his Kentucky muzzleloader, which he had converted from flintlock to percussion.

"You women stay inside and keep the children quite. I'll handle this," he said urgently.

Sitting down on the porch bench he cocked the rifle hammer, slipped on a percussion-firing cap, then lay the gun in his lap and waited.

The riders slid their mounts to a stop in front of the cabin and set their gaze on Lorenzo. Heat from the exhausted horses rose like wisps of smoke, their breath thick in the cool morning air.

"We're looking for James Parker," the forceful leader barked in a gruff voice, eyeing Lorenzo suspiciously. Unlike the other men, who were clothed in homespun tattered trousers, shirt and battered hat, he was dressed in splendid apparel. With an air of authority, he sat tall and erect in the saddle.

"He's not here," James answered.

"Yeah. Well you tell that horse thief we plan to hang him, and if you don't leave this place we're gon'na whip you and destroy all the property. See that he gets the message," the leader demanded before they turned and galloped away.

Inside the house Lorenzo found a frightened and shaky group of women.

"What are we going to do?" Patsey fretted, holding three-year-old Martha tight in her arms with the other children gathered around. "Those men mean to kill my husband."

"Lorenzo you need to find Father and Luther before those men do. They need to be warned," Sarah said desperately.

Rachel, now over seven months pregnant sat quietly by the fireplace, mortified. What had she come home to? During the year since her return there had been constant turmoil. Neighbors suing neighbors. People being killed with little or no proof of wrong doing. Shootings and stabbings for no reason.

Lord, this is not what I prayed to come home to, Rachel thought. *The uneducated Indians live in a more harmonious system of equity. Even when I, a white captive, was caught in a violent fight with my mistress, they allowed me the opportunity to plead my defense to a court of twelve council chiefs before passing sentence. Their civil laws are always settled by a council of chiefs – not by killing each other – and we call them an uncivilized, ignorant race of heathens.*

"You're right Sarah. I need to locate James before those reprobates do," Lorenzo said. "James Wilson, go saddle my horse."

Ten-year-old James shot out the door and was back in about ten minutes. "He's tied out front, saddled and ready to go!" he announced.

Lorenzo slipped on his heavy leather coat, gathered up his saddlebag and rifle and headed for the door. "Be back in about two days, I'll hav'ta skirt around Huntsville and stay clear of the main wagon road to Montgomery. Don't want to meet up with any vigilantes. I'll stop by our neighbor's and ask them to come check on you. Don't think there'll be any trouble here. They're looking for James."

Outside Lorenzo shoved his muzzleloader into the saddle's gun scabbard and swung up in the saddle. A brisk north wind was now blowing, dropping the temperature and bringing a fine mist of rain. He pulled his hat down against the wind and loped off down the road.

* * *

Montgomery, Texas

"James Parker!" a bitter voice called.

James, who was sitting on his horse watching Luther and some other men unload lumber from the wagon, turned in the saddle to see who called his name.

A barrel-bellied man dressed immaculately in a broadcloth suit and stovepipe hat was standing on the porch of the trading post across the road, motioning for James to come over. It had been raining all morning but had now stopped. Supposing the man did not want to muddy his shiny boots, James turned his horse and rode over. James had never met the man but knew him to be William Sheppard, a prosperous local citizen of Montgomery.

"James Parker, you were notoriously known in Illinois to be a counterfeiter and we know you to be not only a counterfeiter here in Texas but a horse thief. Even associating with the very Indians who steal our horses. That horse you are riding is stolen. We don't need folks like you here in Texas!" Sheppard declared loud and belligerently so all within hearing would know.

"Are you William W. Shepperd?" James asked.

"Yes I am!"

"Well Mr. Sheppard, I'm telling you, you just lied to all these people. I'm not guilty of any of those charges!" James stated, then turned his horse and cantered back across the road.

"You stay around here and you'll get yourself hung from a tree!" Sheppard shouted.

"What was that all about?" Luther asked.

"Aw, the man's crazy with arrogant pride. Should file suit against him for slander. There are plenty of witnesses. It's getting late. We better find a place to stay the night. Take the wagon down to the stockyard and feed the mules good before turning them loose. I'll scout around for a place to stay."

* * *

Daylight was fading when Lorenzo rode his exhausted horse into Montgomery. At the far end of the village he could see, what he thought to be, Luther leading the mules into the stock pens. He kicked his horse to a lope in that direction.

"Luther, where is James?" Lorenzo shouted when he neared the pens.

"I'm here." Lorenzo had not seen James ride up. "What are you doing here?"

"Six regulators came to your house early this morning looking for you. Said they were gon'na kill you. Even threatened me!"

"Who were they?"

"Don't know. I've seen a couple of them around Huntsville before. James, those vigilantes mean business. You may want to think about going into hiding for a spell."

"Yeah. I think you're right. Looks like the wind has pushed the rain out and it's going to be a clear night. I'm going to ride home tonight and slip in for supplies tomorrow. Need to let the family know. You two stay the night and start home with the wagon tomorrow. I'm going to send Patsey and the girls to Joseph's home in Houston."

Joseph Parker was James' younger brother and had accumulated vast land holdings near the city of Houston. "Luther you see they get there safely. Lorenzo I think it best if James Wilson stayed with you and Sarah. He'll be a big help to you in watching the place."

Though the road was sloggy, James made good time under a star-lit frosty night and was nearing his home in Parker's Mill at the first gray light of morning. Skirting through the trees he circled within one-hundred-yards to the back of his house. Dismounting, he tied his horse and waited at the edge of the timber.

In the stillness of the crisp cold early morning he watched as curls of smoke rose from the chimney. He could almost feel the warmth of the fire and smell the aroma of fresh baked bread.

Why Lord am I being driven from my home, he thought. *First my children were taken from me and now even some of my friends have turned against me. Why Lord? Can I not ever find peace?*

James was considering making a dash for the house when he saw James Wilson come out and head for the barn. He watched until his son was inside the cow lot before sprinting towards the barn door.

"James Wilson!" James said in a muffled voice, startling his son.

"Father!"

"Is everyone alright in the house?"

"Ye – yes sir."

"Have those men who call themselves the 'Regulators' been back?"

"No sir. But our neighbor told us he thinks they may be watching for you."

"They probably are. I want you to go to the house and tell your mother to bring me a change of clothes and some food, bread and meat. Also, I'll need gun powder and bullets. Tell her to put them in buckets so it will appear she's going to milk the cows. You come back with her."

"Yes sir. Where are you going?"

"I don't know son. Probably up in Indian country. I've got to stay gone 'till this thing blows over. Now go on and tell your mother. And don't run."

James Wilson ambled back to the house just as he did every day after feeding the animals.

About fifteen minutes had passed when James saw his wife and boy coming to the barn where he was waiting, each carrying a bucket.

"James, what are we going to do?" Patsey fretted.

"I'm going in hiding until things settle down. Luther will be here tomorrow and take you and the girls to stay with Joseph in Houston. James Wilson, you're going home with Sarah and Lorenzo. He'll need help in tending to our stock."

"I'm going up in Indian country and search for John and James Pratt. Maybe one of the Indian traders has heard something. Stay in Houston 'till I get back."

"Are you leaving now?" Patsey asked, with a worried frown.

"No. I'm staying here in the barn 'till nightfall and get some rest. I think it's going to be a clear starlit night making easy traveling. I need to put some distance behind me before daylight. Son, my horse is tied in the edge of the woods. I want you to take him a bucket of feed. You can water him at the creek. When you come back bring my saddlebags."

"Yes sir."

"Patsey, I'm not coming to the house. Just tell the girls I'll see them in Houston. When it gets dark send James Wilson with my traveling bedroll and some food. This will all settle down in time. The Lord is just testing our faith right now."

* * *

In the pre-dawn light Luther pulled the mules to a stop near the barn and unhooked them from the wagon. Lorenzo unsaddled his horse and turned him loose in the corral with the mules. The two men picked up their gear out of the wagon and headed for the house.

They had set out from Montgomery early yesterday morning intending to camp for the night along the way. But, as night fell the clear sky came alive with a host of brilliant stars and they traveled on, hoping to make Parker's Mill before daylight.

At first they saw only the light of a burning candle but as they drew near the house the dim outline of James Wilson standing on the porch came into view.

"Is that you Luther?"

"Yeah, it's me and Lorenzo. Thought you might have heard us come in."

"Yeah. We didn't expect you 'till late evening. You must have traveled all night."

Inside the house they found everyone up except three-year-old Martha. Sarah was at the fireplace stirring smoldering coals to set the coffeepot on and kindling a small fire to warm the room.

"You boys sit down and rest," Patsey insisted. "We'll have you something to eat shortly. Probably haven't had much to eat since leaving Montgomery. James left early last night. Said he was going to Indian country to search for our two boys, John and James Pratt."

For the next hour the two men and women sipped hot coffee and discussed plans for the trip to Houston, a distance of over eighty-miles.

Due to Rachel's pregnant and weakening condition and the two children, Frances and Martha, they decided it best to take the wagon. After readying the wagon with a cover and loading supplies they all rested until sundown. If the night was clear Luther, Rachel, her mother, Patsey, and her two children could leave in the wagon and be over ten miles south of Huntsville by daylight, possibly avoiding any confrontation with 'regulators'.

Rachel sat quietly by the sizzling fire, gazing into its' dancing flames, occasionally entering in the conversation, but only halfheartedly.

Lord of Heaven, I sit here watching these flickering flames of fire and realize how quickly dreams of a normal life, free of fears, nightmares and disappointments can disappear like smoke ascending up a chimney, Rachel brooded. *I have endured unspeakable torture and loss off my children. Traveled thousands of miles in worse than terrible conditions. My once healthy, vigorous body has been reduced to a sickly, wasted-away frame, slouched here in this chair. And now dear Father we must flee from our home. Leave family and friends. Travel through the dead of winter to a place and a future filled with uncertainties while my father is being hunted like a criminal by unscrupulous men who seek to kill him. Oh Lord, when will it all end?*

* * *

The tarp-covered wagon bumped and vibrated along the narrow wagon road under the dim blue-light of a half moon. The only sounds to be heard were the rattling of chains, the rhythmical clopping of mules' hooves and an occasional snort by one of the mules or Luther's horse tethered to the back of the wagon.

With a lap quilt wrapped around their legs, Rachel huddled against Luther trying to ward off the near freezing night air. She thought of her long journey across the seemingly endless hot dry plains of New Mexico and Kansas when she yearned only for a cool breeze. But tonight the warm rays of a morning sun could not come soon enough.

Her mother, wrapped in a wool robe, sat in a rope-bottom chair while her two young children slept on pallets on the wagon floor.

Wishing to make good time, the wagon was lightly loaded with only the bare essentials needed for what could be a long stay in Houston. Even then, the two large mules strained to move the wagon up the many hills along the route.

Under the security of darkness the loaded wagon had passed, unnoticed, through the town of Huntsville. And now, six hours later, the travelers were well on their way, feeling free to stop at the first dim light of daybreak for a much needed rest. They would then find a secluded spot to cook up a hot meal while the animals grazed.

Rachel was reflecting on these things when she noticed dark clouds drifting in, hiding the half-moon in a vale of darkness.

"Folks, it looks like we're about to get a little rain," Luther announced. "Rachel step back there and help your mother secure the wagon canvas down tight. The wind has picked up."

At first only a scattering of large heavy drops pelted the tarp. Then came a flash of lightening and a bitter cold north wind, bringing with it diagonal sheets of thrashing rain.

Luther moved from the driver's seat back under the tarp covering. In the dense curtain of rain only the backs of the mules could be seen. "We're going to hav'ta stop," Luther shouted. "Can't see the road. There's a road along here somewhere leading up to the village of Waverly but it's too dark to find it now."

At that moment a streak of lightening lit up the sky revealing the faint outline of a wagon road only a few yards ahead, leading off to the left. Letting the mules feel their way forward, Luther gave a slight tug on the left rein and the wagon soon turned on what he hoped was a road.

As the heavens poured forth, the two mules sloshed up the rain soaked road, with their heavy burden, toward Waverly.

When the wind and rain began to subside a faint yellow light could be seen in the distance. Soon, through the pale light of breaking dawn, the shadowy image of a small log house and barn came into view.

"We'll stop here and see if these folks will allow us to stay in their barn 'till this rain has passed," Luther announced. "Maybe they'll let us warm and dry out by their fire." He could see curls of smoke ascending from the cabin's chimney.

By this time the five fugitives were freezing cold and wet, anxious for the warmth of a blazing fire.

With rain still peppering down Luther hustled briskly to the cabin door, leaving the two women and children in the wagon. His knock was soon answered by a large heavy-boned man with a weathered, wrinkled face under a stubby beard, holding a steaming cup of coffee.

"Uh – Hello young man. Come in out of this cold rain. You by yourself?"

"No sir. My pregnant wife, mother-in-law and two children are out in the wagon. I was wondering sir, if we might impose on you and warm by your fire?"

"Lord yes," the man declared, looking out at the wagon. "Tell them to come on in. You can put your stock in that pen at the barn. Martha! Put on some more coffee. We've got company."

"I'm James Winter and this is my wife Martha," Mr. Winter said when everyone was seated or standing around the fire sipping hot coffee. The two young girls had been given warm milk to drink.

Mrs. Winter was a grandmotherly-looking woman with a big inviting smile that put everyone instantly at ease. "Where are you folks headed?" she asked.

"We live near Huntsville and were on our way to visit my

husband's brother in Houston when we got caught in this rain storm," Patsey answered, but did not give any details about why they were going.

"Well, you're certainly welcome to stay here until the weather clears," Mr. Winter offered. "Looks like the rain has set in for the day."

"Sir, if it's alright with you, we would like to bed down in your barn for some much needed sleep and rest," Luther remarked. "We've been traveling all night."

"That would be fine. Martha will fix you folks up with a hot meal while you're drying out."

"Mr. Plummer, I think your wife needs to stay here near the fire. She doesn't look too well," Mrs. Winter insisted.

It was around noon before the sky cleared bringing out the raw red sun to warm the cold November day. The travelers thanked the Winters for their hospitality and bid them farewell before heading out over the mud packed wagon road. To help ease the load, Luther rode his horse letting Patsey guide the lumbering mules.

On the second day, after leaving the village of Waverly, the family arrived at the crossing of the San Jacinto River. The flooded river forced the group to camp for two days on its' banks before it receded enough to cross.

Finally, after three days of fording creeks and bayous and slogging through saturated bog holes, where wagon wheels sank so deep poles had to be used in prying them out, the travelers arrived at the junction of Buffalo Bayou and White Oak Creek. There they crossed over the bayou to the town of Houston – their destination and place of refuge. It was now the first of December 1838.

Houston, Texas
December 1838 – March 1839

Houston was a bustling city of some 2,000 people when Rachel and her family arrived in December of 1838. Located on the south side of Buffalo Bayou adjacent to the ashes of Harrisburg, a town burnt to the ground by the Mexican Army in April of 1836, Houston supported two theaters, three newspapers, and a jail, along with other commercial businesses. It also housed the Capitol of the Republic of Texas with General Sam Houston as its' first president. On the 10th of December Mirabeau Lamar was elected President and the Capitol moved to Austin.

Still, it was a wild boomtown where lawlessness and disease ran rampant. Hogs and other livestock roamed the dirt streets strewn with rubbish.

Since arriving at her Uncle Joseph Parker's home, Rachel had been mostly bedridden. The long, cold journey from her home in Parker's Mill to Houston had taken its' toll on her already weak body. Even after a week of complete rest, in the comfort of her uncle's large home, she was unable to regain her strength, spending many hours sitting or lying near the warmth of the fireplace. Occasionally, on warm sunny days, Rachel lounged in a swing under an arbor, soaking up long shafts of sunshine beaming through its' leafless vines.

A few days after their arrival in Houston, Rachel asked her uncle to take the narrative she had written of her captivity to the newspaper and see if they would print it. She had worked on her story while in Santa Fe, New Mexico and Missouri and completed it before leaving

Parker's Mill.

Due to the publication of her narrative Rachel received many letters and visitors, offering words of comfort. Being unable to entertain visitors for any length of time, she had to rely on her mother to answer their many questions.

After seeing Rachel and her family safely to Houston, Luther returned to Parker's Mill to see about the livestock and property, and to operate the sawmill.

By the last of December Rachel was completely bedridden and just days away from giving birth to her third child. She longed for her husband, yet knew it was necessary for him to be at Parker's Mill to look after their homestead or else looters would ransack the farm and mill.

As time of delivery grew near she became more anxious for his return, praying he would be there when the baby was born.

Rachel eased herself out of bed and shuffled to a chair by a window where warm rays of sunlight peeked through. For the first day of January it was an exceptionally beautiful clear day.

Looking out the window she watched her little sister, Frances, pull turnips out of the winter garden for their noon meal. Suddenly her sister looked up, dropped the batch of turnips and sprinted toward the house.

"Father's coming! Father's coming!" Frances cried, dashing into the house. "Mother! Father's coming and I think Luther is with him!"

"Thank you Lord," Patsey uttered with gratification, rushing to the door.

"Mother! Is it really Father and Luther?" Rachel called, as tears of joy gathered in her eyes.

"Yes dear. It's really them!"

With rejuvenated energy Rachel stumbled to the door, and with her mother's arm around her, waited on the porch for her husband.

"Oh Luther," she murmured with tear filled eyes, while being helped back inside by her husband. "I'm so glad you're here to see our baby come into the world."

That day Rachel, Luther and the two families of Joseph and James Parker gathered around the dinner table for a scrumptious 'New Year's Day' meal and talked joyfully of the new expected arrival to the family.

"Father, are we going home now that you are here?" Rachel asked.

"I'm afraid it's not safe for me to return at this time. There are still men living around Huntsville who would seek to do me harm. To avoid any encounter in getting here, I had to travel an old wagon road down the east side of the Trinity River to the town of Liberty before crossing the river at Lynchburg. Luther and I just happened to meet up here in Houston. Honey, it may be a long time before I can safely return to Parker's Mill."

For several minutes the family at the table fell silent, each in his own thoughts.

"You people cheer up," James scolded lightheartedly. "These things will pass. There'll be better days ahead. You'll see. Rachel, my sweet daughter, this is the best place for you at this time, here in the security of your Uncle Joseph's home. Now let's all enjoy our 'New Year's' dinner and be happy in what our Heavenly Father has given us."

* * *

"Mother! Mother!" Rachel called from the bedroom. "My water just broke."

Patsey rushed into the room where her daughter stood, holding on to the back of a chair.

"Let's get you cleaned up and back into bed. That baby will be coming soon."

Unlike her experience over two years ago when giving birth to a child alone on a dirt floor of an Indian tent in the far cold reaches of the Rocky Mountains, Rachel now had the comfort of a soft warm bed and a caring mother. Just the fact of being here with family reassured her everything would be OK.

For twelve long hours Rachel suffered with unbearable birthing pains. Thinking both baby and mother may die, Luther borrowed Joseph's buggy and raced to town in hopes of locating a doctor. Finding none, he was directed to an experienced mid-wife who he brought hurriedly back to the farm house where everyone waited anxiously.

One hour later, on January 4, 1839, there was much rejoicing when, the mid-wife placed a squalling Wilson Plummer into his grandmother's waiting arms. Though small, he seemed to be a healthy baby.

Rachel lay with her eyes closed, scarcely able to move or speak.

For the next two months Rachel lingered in poor health. Unable to feed her baby boy from her breast, he grew weaker with the passing of each day, never adapting to the milk of cows.

During her long illness Rachel seldom uttered a word of her sufferings, only saying 'this life holds no attraction for me'. She yearned to walk through the shadow of death into the loving outstretched arms of her Lord and Master – out of a world where men became slaves to heartless abuse, committing heinous atrocities against each other. Where cruelty and mercilessness abound, and love, forgiveness and peace are forgotten. Her only wish was that little James Pratt be delivered from the inhuman bondage of suffering and she might live to see his return. Rachel did not live to see her son again.

"My Holy Father, thy will be done." Rachel murmured. With these final words, on March 19, 1839, she breathed out her spirit to Him who gave it. She was twenty years old.

Her infant son, Wilson Plummer, died two days later, March 21, 1839.

* * *

The following poesy was penned by Rachel just days before her death. *

Ye careless ones, who wildly stroll
On life's uneven tide –
List to the sorrows of my soul,
My heaving bosom hide.

Oh, parents will you lend an ear,
And listen to my grief;

Will you let fall for me one tear,
Or could this give relief?

But, oh, my soul! My darling babe,
Was from my bosom torn,
It lies now in deaths gloomy shade,
And I am left to mourn.

Good LORD, I cried can I endure,
Such sorrow and deep grief,
His Holy Spirit kind and pure,
Give my poor soul relief.

* Rachel Plummer Narrative #21

Garlyn Webb Wilburn

Epilogue

Of the five taken captive from Fort Parker on Thursday, May 19, 1836; Elizabeth Kellogg was brought into Nacogdoches, Texas by Delaware Indians on August 20, 1836 and surrendered back to her family for the sum of $150.00; Rachel Plummer was ransomed back from the Comanche Indians by William Donoho in the summer of 1837. At that time the Comanches were living over 500 to 700 miles north of Santa Fe, New Mexico. Rachel arrived back at her father's house at the settlement of Parker's Mill (near present day Huntsville, Texas) on February 19, 1838, one year and nine months after her capture. Rachel died on March 19, 1839, one year after returning home. She was twenty years old; Rachel's son, James Pratt was brought to Fort Gibson, Oklahoma by Kickapoo Indians on August 23, 1842, over six years after being abducted; John Parker was brought into Fort Gibson, Oklahoma on September 28, 1842. John later returned to the Comanche Indians and presumably lived out his life as a rancher in Mexico; Cynthia Ann Parker lived with the Comanche Indians for almost 25 years and was captured back on December 18, 1860 at the headwaters of the Pease River, Cottle County, Texas. At this time, she was married to the Indian Chief Peta Nocona and had two sons, Quanah and Pecos and one daughter, Prairie Flower (Topasanah). Cynthia Ann died in 1864.

The mass grave site of the five men slain at Fort Parker, Elder John Parker, Benjamin F. Parker, Silas M. Parker, Samuel M. Frost

140

and Robert Frost is marked by a granite slab located in Fort Parker Memorial Park Cemetery, Limestone County, Groesbeck, Texas.

A replica of old Fort Parker has been constructed on the original site, just a few miles north of Groesbeck.

Author's Remarks

In reading "The Rachel Plummer Story" the reader may understandably, be caught-up in tilted contempt of the Comanche Indians. But, upon looking further into history of the United States westward movement, many accounts of inhuman atrocious acts of violence, committed by both Indian and White, can be found. In some cases, Indian against Indian and White against White. Killing, torture and abuse appeared to be commonplace:

Massacre at Sand Creek

On November 29, 1864 Colonel John Chivington, with troops of around 800 launched an unprovoked attack against an encampment of Cheyenne Indians near the flowing stream of Sand Creek in Colorado. During this assault 133 Indians were massacred. Of these, 105 were women and children, the rest were old men. When the smoke cleared the men under Chivington's command meticulously killed all the wounded. Women and children who had surrendered were shot while on their knees screaming for mercy. The dead were then scalped regardless of whether they were men, women or children. Some small infants were carried a distance from the camp site and left on the ground to perish.

Shot nine times, Chief Black Kettle and his wife fled up stream. She was shot and killed but he miraculously escaped and survived.

Afterwards the men dressed their weapons with scalps and other body parts. They especially delighted in publicly displaying their trophies in the Denver saloons and boasting of their brave deeds.

Under congressional investigation Chivington claimed they had killed between 500 and 600 militant Indian warriors.

The truth is, there were no warriors in the village. All young men had left on a buffalo hunt. Colonel Chivington and his men surprised and brutally murdered, in cold blood, the unsuspecting old men, women and children who had every reason to believe they were under the protection of the United States authorities and were even flying an American flag and a flag of truce at the time of the attack.

This is but one of the many heinous crimes carried out by the American people against bands of peaceful Native Americans.

Bibliography

Andreus, Pearl. *Juana, Spanish Girl in Central Texas.* Burnet, Texas: Eakin Press, 1982

Bate, W. N. *Frontier Legend.* New Bern, North Carolina: Owen G. Dunn Co., 1954

Betty, Gerald. *Comanche Society.* Texas A&M, College Station, Texas: University Press, 2002

Bial, Raymond. *The Comanche.* New York, New York: Benchmark Books, 2000

Brown, John Henry. *Indian Wars & Pioneers.* Austin, Texas: Daniell Publishers, 1880

Clark, H. *Comanche Bondage.* Glendale, California: H. Clark Company, 1955

De Shields, James T. *Border Wars of Texas*, Waco, Texas: Texian Press, 1976

De Shield, James T. *Cynthia Ann Parker.* Dallas, Texas: Chama Press, 1991

Dickenson, Alice. *Taken by the Indians, True Tales of Captivity.* New York, New York: Franklin Watts, 1976

Exeley, JoElla Powell. *Frontier Blood.* College Station, Texas: A&M University Press, 2001

George, Charles. *The Comanche.* San Diego, California: Kidhaven Press, 2003

Gonzales, Catherine T. *Cynthia Ann Parker, Indian Captive.* Burnet, Texas: Eakin Press, 1980

Harris, Dilue. *Life In Early Texas, Reminiscences of Mrs. Dilue Harris*: 1833-1839

Holly, Mary Austin. *Texas.* Austin, Texas: The Texas State Historical Association: The University of Texas, 1985

Hunter, John Dunn. *Memoirs of Captivity Among the Indians of North America.* New York, New York: Schocken Books, 1973

Jackson, Grace. *Cynthia Ann Parker.* San Antonio, Texas: The Naybor Co., 1959

Meltzer, Milton. *In Their Words.* New York, New York: Thomas Y. Crowell Co., 1964

Meyer, Carolyn. *Where the Broken Heart Still Beats.* Orlando, Florida: Guliver Books, 1992

Bibliography continued...

Narrative of North American Indian Captives. New York and London: Garland Publishing, Inc. 1977

Nelson, Lee. *Three Years Among the Comanches*. Oklahoma: University of Oklahoma Press, 1967

Plummer, Rachel. *Narrative of the Capture and Subsequent Sufferings of Mrs. Rachel Plummer*. Houston, Texas: Self-published, December 3, 1839 – Copyrighted by E. L. Connally, Waco, Texas: Texian Press, 1968

Plummer, Zula. *Search For Rachel*. Waco, Texas: Texian Press, 1968

Parker, James. *The James W. Parker Narrative*, Houston, Texas: Self Published Pamphlet, January 22, 1838

Parker, James. *The Rachel Plummer Narrative*. Texas: Copyright by Rachel Lofton, Susie Hendrix and Jane Kennedy, 1926

Richardson, Rupert Norval. *The Comanche Barrier to South Plains Settlements*. Glendale, California: The Arthur Clark Company, 1933

Rister, Carl Coke. *Comanche Bondage*. Glendale, California: The Arthur Clark Co., 1955

Robson, Lucia St. Clair. *Ride the Wind*. New York, New York: Ballantine Books, 1982

Russel, Marion Sloan. *Land of Enchantment, Memoirs of Marion Russell Along the Santa Fe Trail*. Albuquerque, New Mexico: The University of New Mexico Press, 1954

Tilghman, Zoe A. *The Eagle of the Comanche*. Oklahoma City, Oklahoma: Halow Publishing Corp., 1938

Tolbert, Frank X. *Informal History of Texas*. New York, New York: Harper, 1961

About the Author

Garlyn Webb Wilburn is a native Texan, born in Limestone County, not far from the original site of "Old" Fort Parker.

Following thirty years as a teacher and administrator in Texas public schools, he now lives in Brenham, Texas, where he spends his time writing Texas novels and seeing after his two donkeys. He is the author of three fiction novels: *The Donkey Boy*, *Monday*, and *Désirée's Quest for Freedom*.

.